Programme Text

C000293101

Hou

by Beru Tessema

||SAMUEL FRENCH||

USE OF COPYRIGHTED MUSIC

A licence issued by Concord Theatricals to perform this play does not include permission to use the incidental music specified in this publication. In the United Kingdom: Where the place of performance is already licensed by the PERFORMING RIGHT SOCIETY (PRS) a return of the music used must be made to them. If the place of performance is not so licensed then application should be made to PRS for Music (www.prsformusic.com). A separate and additional licence from PHONOGRAPHIC PERFORMANCE LTD (www.ppluk.com) may be needed whenever commercial recordings are used. Outside the United Kingdom: Please contact the appropriate music licensing authority in your territory for the rights to any incidental music.

USE OF COPYRIGHTED THIRD-PARTY MATERIALS

Licensees are solely responsible for obtaining formal written permission from copyright owners to use copyrighted third-party materials (e.g., artworks, logos) in the performance of this play and are strongly cautioned to do so. If no such permission is obtained by the licensee, then the licensee must use only original materials that the licensee owns and controls. Licensees are solely responsible and liable for clearances of all third-party copyrighted materials, and shall indemnify the copyright owners of the play(s) and their licensing agent, Concord Theatricals Ltd., against any costs, expenses, losses and liabilities arising from the use of such copyrighted third-party materials by licensees.

IMPORTANT BILLING AND CREDIT REQUIREMENTS

If you have obtained performance rights to this title, please refer to your licensing agreement for important billing and credit requirements.

HOUSE OF IFE was first produced at the Bush Theatre in London, England on 29 April, 2022. The cast was as follows:

SOLOMON.. Jude Akuwudike
TSION..Yohanna Ephrem
MERON.. Sarah Priddy
AIDA.. Karla-Simone Spence
YOSI ....Michael Workeye

The creative team was as follows:

DIRECTOR .... Lynette Linton
SET & COSTUME DESIGNER .... Frankie Bradshaw
LIGHTING DESIGNER ....Jai Morjaria
SOUND DESIGNER & COMPOSER .... Duramaney Kamara
MOVEMENT DIRECTOR .... Kane Husbands
ASSISTANT DIRECTOR .... Monaé Robinson
DRAMATURG .... Deirdre O'Halloran
CASTING DIRECTOR ....Heather Basten CDG
CASTING ASSISTANT ....Fran Cattaneo
FIGHT DIRECTOR..Kate Waters
COSTUME SUPERVISOR.............................. Malena Arcucci
VOICE & DIALECT COACH.................................... Joel Trill
PORTRAIT ARTIST.. Florence Lee
PRODUCTION MANAGER .... Pete Rickards
COMPANY STAGE MANAGER............................Crystal Gayle
ASSISTANT STAGE MANAGER .... Helen Potter

CAST

Jude Akuwudike – SOLOMON

Jude plays the titular role in the feature film *Eyimofe* which premiered at Berlin Film Festival. Other film credits include *Beasts Of No Nation* (dir. Cary Fukunaga), *The Tempest, Touched By A Stranger, Sahara* and *A World Apart* and the forthcoming Disney remake of *The Little Mermaid*.

Jude's television appearances include *Gangs of London* (Sky Atlantic), *Fortitude* (Amazon), *In The Long Run* (Sky One) and *The Crown* (Netflix). Other TV credits include *Manhunt, Chewing Gum, Friday Night Dinner, Cucumber* and the UK version of *Law & Order*.

Having trained at RADA, Jude has performed in productions including Inua Ellams' *Three Sisters* and *Moon On A Rainbow Shawl* (National), *The Convert* (Young Vic), *The Faith Machine* (Royal Court), *Great Expectations* (English Touring Theatre) and *Othello* (Glasgow Citizens). He most recently appeared at the Donmar in *Henry V* with Kit Harrington.

Yohanna Ephrem – TSION

Yohanna's theatre appearances include *Stacked* and *From The Ground Up* (Almeida Youth Company), *Homegrown* and *Skunk* (National Youth Theatre), *Scottsboro Boys Parallel Production* (Young Vic) and *Feather Boy* (National Youth Studio). On television she has appeared in *The Feed* (Amazon Studios), *The Rook* (Starz/Lionsgate) and *Damned* (Channel 4). Her film appearances include *Surge* and *Sweetness in the Belly*.

Sarah Priddy – MERON

Sarah Priddy was born in Britain and raised in the Bahamas by an English father and Sierra Leonean mother. She worked in the advertising industry before embarking on her professional acting career in 2015.

Sarah studied drama at City Lit and trained with Actors Studio, The Mono Box and at RADA. Her acting career began as a supporting artist on several BBC, ITV and Channel 4 TV productions. Her film debut was in Callum Crawford's *Degenerates*. Sarah's stage credits include *The Regina Monologues, Building the Wall, Poison* and *The Deep Blue Sea*. She performed in KatAlyst Productions' *Beginnings* festival in 2020 and is currently working with writer Andrew Sharpe for his new play *The House at the End of Empire*. She was Executive Producer on the short film, *I Am Your Sister*. Later this year she will appear as Mary Dawson in Warren Dudley's feature film *Six Years Gone*.

Karla-Simone Spence – AIDA

Karla-Simone has just filmed the titular role in ITV's *The Confessions of Frannie Langton* and played the lead female in the *Blue Story*, Rapman's feature film, in collaboration with Paramount and BBC Films. Prior to *Blue Story*, she appeared in *Gold Digger* (BBC1) and *Wannabe* (BBC3).

Michael Workeye – YOSI

Since graduating from Arts Educational drama school, Michael's television appearances have included *Sitting in Limbo* (BBC), *Big Age* (Channel 4) and *This is Going To Hurt* (BBC).

CREATIVE TEAM

Beru Tessema – WRITER

Beru Tessema is a film and theatre maker based in London. He trained as an actor at RADA and as a screenwriter at the London Film School. *House of Ife* is his debut work for the stage.

Lynette Linton – DIRECTOR

Director Lynette Linton took over as Artistic Director of the Bush Theatre in 2019.

She directed the UK premiere of Lynn Nottage's Pulitzer Prize-winning play *Sweat* (Donmar Warehouse, Gielgud Theatre) for which she won 'Best Director' at the inaugural Black British Theatre awards. *Sweat* also won the Evening Standard award for 'Best Play' and was nominated for an Oliver award for 'Best New Play'. Her production of *Richard II* (Shakespeare's Globe) which she directed with Adjoa Andoh, marked the first ever company of women of colour in a Shakespeare play on a major UK stage.

Lynette will make her National Theatre debut directing a new production of American writer Pearl Cleage's *Blues for an Alabama Sky* in the Lyttelton from September 2022. *My Name is Leon*, her directorial film debut, will be released on BBC in May 2022. She is co-founder of theatre and film production company, Black Apron Entertainment.

As a writer, her credits include *Look at Me* (ITV), *Hashtag Lightie* (Arcola), *Chicken Palace* and *Step* (Theatre Royal Stratford East).

Her other directing credits include an adaptation of Jackie Kay's *Chiaroscuro* (Bush Theatre), world premiere productions of *Assata Taught Me* (Gate), *Function* (National Youth Theatre), *This Is* (Arts Ed), *Indenture* (Dark Horse Festival), *Naked* (VAULT Festival), and a revival of *This Wide Night* (Albany). She was also co-director on Chicken Palace (Theatre Royal Stratford East).

Frankie Bradshaw – SET & COSTUME DESIGNER

Frankie Bradshaw is an award winning set and costume designer for theatre and performance. She won the Best Creative West End Debut at the Stage Debut Awards 2019 jointly with director Lynette Linton for *Sweat* at the Gielgud Theatre. She was a Jerwood Young Designer in 2017, she won the Off West-End Best Set Design award in 2016, and was a Linbury prize finalist in 2015. Frankie's recent design credits for theatre include: *Sweat* (West End/Donmar Warehouse), *Two Trains Running* (Royal & Derngate/UK Tour), *Cinderella* (Lyric Hammersmith), *A Christmas Carol* (Theatre Clwyd), *Napoli Brooklyn* (UK Tour/Park Theatre), *Skellig* (Nottingham Playhouse), *Trying It On* (UK Tour/RSC/ Royal Court), *Kiss Me Kate, Jerusalem, Nesting, Robin Hood* (Watermill Theatre), *Cookies* (Theatre Royal Haymarket), *On The Exhale* (Traverse), *Hansel* (Salisbury Playhouse). For opera she has designed: *Macbeth, Idomeneo* and *Elizabetta* for English Touring Opera.

Jai Morjaria – LIGHTING DESIGNER

Jai Morjaria trained at RADA and won the 2016 Association of Lighting Designer's ETC Award.

Recent designs include *Wuthering Heights* (Bristol Old Vic/National Theatre); *Cherry Jezebel* (Liverpool Everyman); *Lava, Pawn/Limbo* (Bush Theatre); *Cruise* (Duchess Theatre); *Big Big Sky, The Hoes* (Hampstead Theatre); *My Son's A Queer (But What Can You Do?)* (Turbine Theatre. WhatsOnStage Award for Best Off West End Production); *Hushabye Mountain* (Hope Mill); *Out of the Dark* (Rose Theatre Kingston); *Shuck'n'Jive, Whitewash* (Soho Theatre); *Anansi the Spider, Aesop's Fables* (Unicorn Theatre); *I'll Take You To Mrs. Cole* (Complicite); *Mapping Brent* (Kiln Theatre); *Glory* (Duke's Theatre/Red Ladder); *Cuzco* (Theatre503); *Losing Venice* (Orange Tree Theatre); *The Sorcerer's Apprentice* (Northern Stage); *A Lie of the Mind* (Southwark Playhouse); *46 Beacon* (Trafalgar Studios with Rick Fisher); *Out There on Fried Meat Ridge Road* (White Bear Theatre/Trafalgar Studios 2); *Acorn* (Courtyard Theatre, Off-West End Award nomination for Best Lighting).

Duramaney Kamara – SOUND DESIGNER & COMPOSER

Duramaney Kamara was the composer, sound designer and resident DJ for *Dismantle*, a festival of work by Project 2036 at the Bush Theatre.

As music and sound designer, his credits for the Royal Court include: *My Mum's a Twat* and *Instructions For Correct Assembly*. As composer and sound designer, for the Royal Court: *Katzenmusik* (Young Court); *Tottenham Symphony* (Beyond the Court).

As performer, his theatre credits include: *Boy* (Almeida); *The Response* (Seagull/Mercury). As performer, film credits include: *Yardie, What Happened to Evie*.

Kane Husbands – MOVEMENT DIRECTOR

Kane Husbands is the founder and artistic director of The PappyShow and a lecturer at Central Saint Martins, University of the Arts London. His work is all about community and bringing people together to move, share practice and play. He is a facilitator, director, performer and maker specialising in movement, dance, ensemble and physical theatre. An associate of the National Youth Theatre, Squint Theatre and The North Wall (Oxford). He choreographed the Welcoming Ceremonies of the London Olympics, Paralympics, and the Glasgow Commonwealth Team.

He has worked across National Theatre, Chichester Festival Theatre, Nottingham Playhouse, Sheffield Crucible Theatre, the Old Vic, the Midlands Arts Centre (Birmingham), the SCOOP Outdoor Theatre, Rose Bruford College (London), the Royal Central School of Speech and Drama (London), University of West London, the Royal Welsh College of Music and Drama (Cardiff), the National Youth Theatre, the King Abdulaziz Centre for World Culture (Saudi Arabia), the National Theatre of Scotland and the Kiln Theatre (London) and Fran Wen, among other companies and venues.

For The PappyShow, Kane has directed *BOYS*; *Boy, Fly, Girls (2018)*, *Care, Shine Black, Our House* and *What Do You See?* and continues to lead and curate The PappyShow's works and training in collaboration with the full core team.

Monaé Robinson – ASSISTANT DIRECTOR

Monaé Robinson is the recipient of the Resident Director Bursary programme at the Bush Theatre, working closely with the Artistic team to bring to life their creative visions. She started her career as a community and cultural arts leader. She was recently Assistant Director on *Red Pitch* (Bush Theatre) and *For Black Boys...* (Royal Court).

Monaé holds a Bachelor's degree in Theatre & Performance from Goldsmiths University, and is a performance maker that typically focuses on Afrofuturism. In October 2021, Monaé directed *OJA* as part of Theatre Peckham's Young, Gifted and Black festival.

Deirdre O'Halloran – DRAMATURG

Deirdre O'Halloran is the Literary Manager at the Bush Theatre, working to identify and build relationships with new writers, commission new work and guide plays to the stage. At the Bush she's dramaturged plays including Olivier Award winner *Baby Reindeer* by Richard Gadd, *The High Table* by Temi Wilkey and *An Adventure* by Vinay Patel. Deirdre was previously Literary Associate at Soho Theatre, where she worked as a dramaturg on plays including *Girls* by Theresa Ikoko and *Fury* by Phoebe Eclair-Powell. She led on Soho Theatre's Writers' Lab programme and the biennial Verity Bargate Award. As a freelancer, Deirdre has also been a reader for Out of Joint, Sonia Friedman Productions and Papatango.

Heather Basten CDG – CASTING DIRECTOR

Heather Basten is an English casting director based in London, and a member of the Casting Directors Guild (UK), and the Casting Society of America (USA). In 2021 she was recognised as a Screen International 'Star of Tomorrow', and in 2022 named a BAFTA Breakthrough member.

Heather has cast the upcoming 6-Episode musical TV series, *Jungle* for Amazon Studios and *Dreaming Whilst Black* for the BBC. She has most recently cast the Stone Age-set film *The Origin*, which is the sophomore feature from UK producer Oliver Kassman (Saint Maud), *Red Pitch* and *Fair Play* (both Bush Theatre). Heather is currently casting a new exciting slate of green-lit film and TV series across the BFI, Film 4, BBC and more.

Kate Waters – FIGHT DIRECTOR

Kate Waters' theatre credits include: Regular work at the National Theatre, RSC, Donmar, The Globe and in the West End. She has also worked inmany of the country's regional theatres. Recent work includes *Macbeth* (Almeida), *Small Island* (National), *Henry V* (Donmar), *Cyrano de Bergerac* (West End, Glasgow & Brooklyn), *Tina, The Musical* (West End & Germany), *Sweat* (Donmar & West End).

Television & Film include: *Coronation Street, Emmerdale* and *Hollyoaks* on all of which she is a regular fight director. She has recently filmed *My*

Policeman (Amazon Studios), *Death of England* (Sky Arts & National Theatre – BAFTA Nominee for Best Single Drama), *Romeo & Juliet* (Sky Arts, PBS America & National Theatre), *Gym* (RADA, Short Film). Other film work includes *Pondlife* and *Making Noises Quietly* (Open Palm Films).

She is also a qualified boxing coach and coaches at Rathbone Amateur Boxing Club.

Malena Arcucci – COSTUME SUPERVISOR

Born and raised in Buenos Aires, Argentina, Malena Arcucci is a performance maker currently based in London. She uses devised and physical theatre techniques, in combination with her background and interest in costume making and sculpture to explore new forms of storytelling. She currently works as a producer and theatre designer, and is co-artistic director of Mariana Malena Theatre Company.

Design credits include: *Friday Night Love Poem* (Zoo Venues Edinburgh); *Point of No Return* (Actor's Centre), *La Llorona* (Dance City Newcastle); *The Two of Us* (Theatre Deli); *Playing Latinx* (Camden's People's Theatre); and various productions in Buenos Aires, Argentina.

Associate Designer credits include: *Dear Elizabeth* (Gate); *Chiaroscuro* (Bush Theatre); *Thebes Land* and *Tamburlaine* (Arcola).

Costume Supervisor and Maker credits include: *Moreno* and *Milk and Gall* (Theatre503); *The Phantom of the Opera* (Her Majesty's Theatre); *Raya* (Hampstead Theatre), amongst others.

Joel Trill – VOICE & DIALECT COACH

Joel Trill's recent work in theatre includes: *The 47th, A Number* and *Bagdad Cafe* (Old Vic); *All My Sons* and *As You Like It* (Queens Theatre Hornchurch); *Statements After An Arrest Under The Immorality Act* (Orange Tree); *Love Letters* (Queens Theatre); *J'Ouvert* (Harold Pinter); *Mirror Mirror, Master Harold and The Boys* (National); *Rockets & Blue Lights* (Royal Exchange); *Trojan Horse* (Battersea Arts Centre); *A Taste of Honey* (Trafalgar Studios); *Two Trains Runnin* (Royal & Derngate); *Red Dust Road* (National Theatre of Scotland); *Strange Fruit* (Bush Theatre); *One Night in Miami* (Nottingham Playhouse); *The Glass Menagerie* (Arcola).

Film & TV: *The White Lotus, Riches, The Confessions Of Frannie Langton, Gangs of London* (Season 2), *The Crown* (Season 5), *Citadel, My Name is Leon, Empire, The Ancestors, Queen & Slim, Mama Ks Team 4, There's Something About The Movies.*

Bush Theatre 50

EST. 1972

We make theatre for London. Now.

Celebrating its 50th Birthday in 2022, the Bush is a world-famous home for new plays and an internationally renowned champion of playwrights. We discover, nurture and produce the best new writers from the widest range of backgrounds from our home in a distinctive corner of west London.

The Bush has won over 100 awards and developed an enviable reputation for touring its acclaimed productions nationally and internationally.

We are excited by exceptional new voices, stories and perspectives – particularly those with contemporary bite which reflect the vibrancy of British culture now.

Located in the newly renovated old library on Uxbridge Road in the heart of Shepherd's Bush, the theatre houses two performance spaces, a rehearsal room and the lively Library Café & Bar.

Supported by
ARTS COUNCIL ENGLAND   h&f hammersmith & fulham

bushtheatre.co.uk

THANK YOU

The Bush Theatre would like to thank all its supporters whose valuable contributions have helped us to create a platform for our future and to promote the highest quality new writing, develop the next generation of creative talent, lead innovative community engagement work and champion diversity.

Supported by
ARTS COUNCIL ENGLAND

If you are interested in finding out how to be involved, please visit **bushtheatre.co.uk/support-us** or email **development@bushtheatre.co.uk** or call **020 8743 3584**.

Bush Theatre

CHARACTERS

AIDA – (29) Ife's twin sister
TSION – (23) her sister
YOSI – (19) their brother
MERON – (52) their mother
SOLOMON – (61) their father

SETTING

London

TIME

The action takes place in July, during a heatwave, in present day.

AUTHOR'S NOTES

Pronunciation: Ife / [aɪːf] / eyef

A slash (/) indicates overlapping dialogue.

Where there is no punctuation, it indicates a continuation of the character's thought, action or intention.

For the loved ones we lost along the way.
Home is always within us.

Love, Eyu.

1.

(A hot and humid Sunday afternoon in July. Kentish Town, North West London.)

(A ground floor council flat living room that leads to a partially open-plan kitchen and a hallway that leads to the front door. Light from the blazing day outside pours in through the recently installed double glazed windows. An extendable dining table occupies one side of the space near the kitchen. A large couch covered in see-through plastic is in front of the TV on the other side of the room. Framed Biblical quotes, Ethiopian ornaments and photographs of the family in happier times hang on the walls. We get the sense that the family has lived here for many years, the evidence of these years are apparent in the worn, faded, cluttered objects and details in the space.)

*(**AIDA**, dressed in black clothes that suggests a keen fashion sense, lights some frankincense and ritualistically spreads the smoke around the room. She places the frankincense on the windowsill then goes outside. Some moments later, she haphazardly carries a stack of chairs inside. **TSION**, also in black clothing, but more ordinary than her sister, arranges a buffet of Ethiopian food on the dining table and returns to the kitchen. The sounds and aromas of Tsion's cooking spills out into the living room area. **TSION** brings more food out*

to the table. **AIDA** *glances at* **TSION** *as though
she wants to say something.* **TSION** *notices
and goes over to comfort her.)*

*(***YOSI** *enters the space. He is awkward in
his body, not yet a man, but charismatic,
with the air of invincibility of youth about
him. He wears a designer pouch across his
chest, an ironed black shirt, light grey jeans
and box-fresh white trainers. His jeans and
trainers both have grass stains on them.)*

YOSI. That was propa long man! Oi, is Dad here yet?

TSION. Fam, where are they?

YOSI. He's not here? Yo? Did Dad call? Has he called yet?

AIDA. Can't get through to / him.

YOSI. What?

AIDA. Dad.

YOSI. Swear down when Dad gets here yeah, that
Preacher's gonna get it. Truss. Man was out there all
tryin' ta hold people hostage with his faf / ya know.

TSION. Bruv?

YOSI. Yo, man was making a scene innit, you know one
of dem ones there? Man juss misjudged the occasion
ya get me, like, man thinks people wanna stay on their
knees listening to him gassin' in this heat / bruv!

AIDA. What? He gave another / sermon?

YOSI. Oi, that brea was movin' like some false prophet out
there fam!

TSION. Oi / bruv?

YOSI. Nah, we was on our way back innit – out of nowhere
man like him starts wilin' out like he was touched by
the Spirit! Made us all fuckin' kneel bruv! Fucked up

my garms ya know! Look at that! Fucking grass on my True Religions brevs! Propa fuckeries innit? Fucked up my creps too innit! Look at that! / Dickhead!

TSION. Are they coming / or what?

YOSI. That's why I don't go to Church ya get me! Since Dad left it's been full of man like that movin' off-key / fam!

TSION. This boy / man!

AIDA. What? Are they still / there?

YOSI. Mum couldn't even kneel like that ya get me, bare people trying to hold her up, and that brea was juss there wilin' out, thinkin' he can juss spit another sermon on road, swear down, pissing / me off!

TSION. So you just left Mum on her own?

YOSI. Like, man juss made the whole ting about him innit. Tone def. Propa tone def fam. His voice was juss grating on me. I had to bounce ca I weren't lookin' to switch ya get me. Then I mussa seen some hoodrats from Crescent. Dem man tried filming us innit. I was fuming bruv. Dem man all started creasing when we knelt down, like it was some joke ting. Swear down, next time I see dem wasteyuts, watch what happens! / Watch!

TSION. Wait. What? You left Mum coz some Crescent heads / saw you?

YOSI. Yo, that Preacher got shook when I juss bowled past him! He got prang innit!

TSION. Yosh man! / Fucking hell!

YOSI. What?

TSION. You were supposed to be with her! That was all. One thing, that's all you had to do fam!

YOSI. Shut up / man!

TSION. Seriously bruv! You need to fix up ya know!

AIDA. You don't need to be getting caught up in all that hood shit Yosi. Don't be an idiot.

YOSI. Idiot?

AIDA. It's not what I / mean

YOSI. *(Like a Yard Man.)* What? Fam, if I'm an "idiot", yuh ah eediat! Yah seh meh?

TSION. Oi, you two, don't start, / yeah!

AIDA. I'm juss saying forget all this roadman bullshit and go be with her. We got it covered / here.

YOSI. Bare people are with her. She told me to come give you lot a hand / innit.

TSION. So you didn't "bowl past" no one then did you?

YOSI. Shut up man! Oi, where's Dad man? Shall we bell him?

AIDA. Yosh, we have to get the place ready / yeah!

YOSI. "We"? Brevs, I don't see you doing no cooking so hol' it down yeah.

TSION. Yosh, you're not / helping!

AIDA. Bruv, don't try chatting to me like you're some badman when you're the one running from Crescent heads! Allow / it!

YOSI. Look at you tryin' to talk road!

AIDA. Whatever Yosi / man.

YOSI. Yo, when's Dad / reaching?

TSION. We don't know bruv!

> *(AIDA checks her phone and goes to check outside the front door that has been left open.)*

YOSI. Oi T, that smells good man!

(He goes to fix himself a plate, **TSION** *smacks his arm and takes away his plate.* **YOSI** *kisses his teeth.)*

What you doing?!

TSION. You can eat when they get here bruv.

YOSI. Pagan! *(Checks his phone.)*

TSION. *(To both* **YOSI** *and* **AIDA.)** We're gonna need more chairs than that ya know. Did you see how many of them there were?

YOSI. He told me he was gonna touch down this morning / fam.

TSION. He'll get here when he gets here innit. A plane has already landed from Addis this morning. I don't know what's happened to him.

YOSI. Nah, fuckeries man.

*(***YOSI*** *goes into the kitchen and pours himself some cereal and starts munching.)*

TSION. *(To* **AIDA.)** Is that all the neighbours had? *(To* **YOSI.)** How far are / they?

AIDA. Yeah, this was all their chairs.

YOSI. Oi, do you lot reckon Dad got caught up in the madness out / there?

TSION. How about the garden ones? You know the old ones in the shed?

YOSI. Auntie Genet was there, did you lot see her? She landed this morning and still reached on time so where is he fam?

TSION. Yosh man, can't you see we're trying to sort this place out before they get here? Why you juss standing / there?

YOSI. What? Yo! Who you chattin' / to?

TSION. Can you at least get the chairs from the shed?!

YOSI. Why they even comin' in here? They should all juss cotch outside. It's a nice day / innit.

TSION. *(To* **YOSI.***)* Fam can you juss get the garden chairs from the shed and clean them up / a bit.

YOSI. Hangers on innit. I ain't even seen half of them before.

TSION. Yeah, it's coz you don't go to Church bruv.

YOSI. Why we stressing about where they sit? Let them perch out there or whatever.

TSION. That's not our culture bruv, ya get me, I don't want to embarrass her again. It was bad enough this morning.

YOSI. It's them dusty ass garden chairs thass gonna embarrass her. We don't even have no garden but somehow all that bruck-up garden furniture been taking up bare space in that shed from day dot.

TSION. What do you call that out there?

YOSI. Bruv, that ain't no / garden!

TSION. That's still a garden to Mum.

AIDA. We used to have them garden chairs around the dining table.

YOSI. Rah! Fam, you lot were on some broke nigga shit then innit!

AIDA. Ridiculous!

YOSI. What?

AIDA. You.

YOSI. Nah, I ain't about that broke life, ya feel / me?

AIDA. But you're still living at yard and working at Sainsbury's, so don't be chatting like you're Nipsey Hussle coz you / ain't!

YOSI. Nah, why you hatin' / fam?

TSION. You lot! Come on man!

> (**TSION** *takes her phone and stands at the window as she makes a call.*)

YOSI. They're all going on like they knew Ife, like they loved Ife, but when he was here they'd cross the road to avoid him ya get me! That's how you / know innit!

AIDA. Like you didn't do that as well yeah?

YOSI. What do you mean like I didn't / do that?

TSION. She's not answering / her phone.

AIDA. Go on like you didn't know him.

YOSI. Fam, *you're* trying to lecture me about Ife?

TSION. Seriously, you lot need to stop beefing and give me a hand! They're gonna be here any minute / now!

> (**TSION** *goes back into the kitchen.*)

AIDA. Yosi man, move from / me.

YOSI. If you were gonna be too shook to speak in front of people why did you even get up there in the first place bruv? That shit was embarrassing / fam!

AIDA. At least I got up there. You couldn't even stay with Mum when that's all you had to do / today.

YOSI. Yeah, what? You got up and couldn't even speak bruv! This is you up there fam...

> (**YOSI** *does an impression of* **AIDA** *struggling to speak on the pulpit.*)

AIDA. You're a / dickhead.

YOSI. What? Did you forget his name or / something?

AIDA. Yosi man, you're pissing me off now! Come out my face man!

TSION. *(From the kitchen.)* Oi, Yosh, can you lot get those fucking chairs already?!

YOSI. I ain't tryin' to deep it yeah, I'm juss playing yeah.

AIDA. Grow the fuck / up!

YOSI. Real talks yeah, Ife was begging outside that Church, begging on road innit, and them lot went on like they didn't even know man, and now look at them! All trying to come through and start crying and / shit!

TSION. Fam, what do you think they were doing all those evenings they come here? They were praying for him. All the mothers of the Church prayed for him all the time so juss allow it yeah.

> *(TSION goes back into the kitchen. AIDA sprays and wipes down some chairs.)*

YOSI. *(To AIDA.)* Yo Aida, you alright?

AIDA. I'm fine.

YOSI. What? We bless yeah?

AIDA. It's fine Yosi man. I just need to get through today.

YOSI. Yo, you wanna bun a likle zoot before them lot get here?

AIDA. Yes, Yosi! Ah, that's exactly what I need. What you got?

YOSI. Green innit. Natural tings fam. Nothing loud ya get me.

> *(YOSI starts to roll a spliff.)*

AIDA. Let's finish sorting all this out and go up on the roof then.

YOSI. Fam! You know that's the spot innit.

> *(TSION comes in looking dismayed.)*

TSION. Bruv where did you put the plates?

YOSI. In the cupboard innit.

TSION. Bruv, you better put that away before they get here!

(**TSION** *goes back to the kitchen.*)

YOSI. *(To* **AIDA.***)* I go up there and fuckin' survey the manor innit.

(**TSION** *comes back in.*)

TSION. This?!

YOSI. Huh?

TSION. Bruv, these birthday ones are the only paper ones in there!

YOSI. Nah, I thought...

TSION. Bro swear down seriously – don't tell me you forgot to get the plates I asked for?!

YOSI. No one's gonna notice.

TSION. What do you mean no one's gonna notice? That's all I asked you to sort out yesterday!

YOSI. I juss...you know what it is yeah... / it was

TSION. *(Giving some money to* **YOSI.***)* Can you run down to the shops and get some?

YOSI. I wanna be here if Dad calls innit!

TSION. Now!

YOSI. I wanna chat to him. See if he's alright and / that.

TSION. Bruv you're wearing my patience thin you know! Couldn't even do the one thing I asked you to do! Come on man. Hurry up!

YOSI. *(Kissing his teeth and putting the rolled spliff behind his ear.)* Nah, you take the piss fam!

(YOSI *meanders in the hallway, scrolling on his phone.*)

TSION. Are you going or what?

YOSI. Alright. Alright. Chill, I'm going! (*Almost to himself.*) This some fuckeries man!

(YOSI *exits.*)

TSION. Swear down that boy!

(*Beat.*)

AIDA. We should have buried him back home. That's what he would have wanted you know.

TSION. I know fam.

AIDA. We should go. When this war is over we should go and spend like half the year out there. I miss it so much.

TSION. Dad's finished building that house out there innit. We should definitely go fam.

AIDA. Mum was saying I can do my work there when things calm down. I could turn one of the rooms into a studio, you can turn another room into a little school or something. You can teach the local kids out there and I can paint, and Mum can have the top floor and we'll have all that land to grow our own food and live properly. That's where we should be you know. That would do us so much good.

TSION. Fam, I'm on that!

AIDA. I want to paint you in that Ethiopian light / T.

TSION. Ethiopian light yeah?

AIDA. The light is different over there T, it's like purple and gold, and at night it's this orange moon that makes everything glow. And when the stars come out, they cover the whole sky. Me and Ife used to stare out the window at night counting shooting stars.

TSION. Rah, you make it sound like some Disney shit fam, can't wait to go back there again!

AIDA. *(Referring to a framed photo on the wall)* In that shack where we lived me and Ife used to have endless adventures. So close to nature. Music was everywhere back then...

TSION. Is it?

AIDA. We had this corrugated iron roof that sung when the sun would heat it up.

TSION. Rah!

AIDA. And behind our shack it was that garden T! See it? This... this... insanely beautiful wild garden! It was... it was magical you know.

>   *(Beat.)*

AIDA. We were so full back then, me and Ife. We were so full.

TSION. Musta been mad to go from that to this.

AIDA. It was...

TSION. You lot are still lucky to have had that though.

AIDA. That shack was our happy home. Wish you coulda seen it, T.

TSION. I wanna go fam. I wanna go back again and see if that garden is still there.

AIDA. Let's do it then. This time next year, if things calm down, me and you T.

>   *(Beat.)*

TSION. It's gonna be too many people to have in here don't you think?

AIDA. I know. Why don't we just move the table and chairs outside?

TSION. Do you reckon Mum would mind?

AIDA. She won't. It's better like that. We can just move the table out there, they're gonna bring more food as well you know.

TSION. Alright then, let's move all this first. Auntie Zawde brought all this wot man, I don't even know if there will be enough injera.

> (**AIDA** *and* **TSION** *move some dishes and pots off the table.*)

Neighbours might get pissed though.

AIDA. They ain't gonna say anything.

TSION. If they complain just give them some / *doro wot* innit!

AIDA. Shut them up with some spice!

TSION. Yeah, you done know!

> (*They giggle for a moment and then fall silent.*)

I hope he's alright. Dad. It's mad innit, the war's been going on for two years and he's all up in it.

AIDA. He's in the city. Mum said life is just carrying on like normal in the city.

TSION. Still, can't believe he's out there and that's happening.

AIDA. Do you reckon Mum's gonna be alright letting him stay here?

TSION. Where else is he going to stay?

AIDA. He's still got his friend in Tottenham hasn't he?

TSION. Oh yeah, his bredrin' with that yard with all Bible pages stuck on the windows!

AIDA. That place is creepy as fuck!

TSION. Like that priest's room from *The Omen* fam!

AIDA. Ah, that film usta get me so shook ya know!

TSION. Yeah and Dad made us watch it coz he thought it was educational!

> (**AIDA** *stands at the window and looks out at the estate.*)

That boy! How long is he gonna be?!

> (**TSION** *offers* **AIDA** *some injera.*)

What do you reckon?

AIDA. Yeah, that's really good T!

> (*In the distance we can hear the boisterous banter of* **YOSI** *and some local boys.*)

TSION. (*Calling for* **YOSI** *at the door.*) OI, YOSH! YOSI!! This boy man!! YOSH!!

> (**TSION***'s phone rings, she quickly answers.*)

Daddy...?

> (**AIDA** *rushes over to listen to the conversation.* **TSION** *puts her phone on speaker...*)

SOLOMON. Tsionie!

TSION. Daddy? Daddy where are you?

> (*He speaks in a panicked and urgent way at the top of his voice.*)

SOLOMON. Addis... I am still in Addis Tsionie...? Tsionie can you hear me? Tsion are your brother and sister there?

TSION. Yes they're / here Daddy.

AIDA. (*Taking the phone.*) Why are you still in Addis?

(A child screams in the background on
SOLOMON*'s line.)*

SOLOMON. Aida... Oh Aida! Aida! Hello?

AIDA. Dad, you missed the funeral!

SOLOMON. Huh? Aidiyay? Aida? Huh? Can you hear me?

AIDA. Yes, I can hear you Dad, can you get the next plane?

SOLOMON. Ah, Aida, these people! They are corrupt! Ah! I am in hell here! Do you hear me Aida? Hello? Aida, they canceled the airplane and now... now these people.. they refuse to refund me! They stole my money! They swindled / me!

cancelled

TSION. / Dad just calm down it's okay.

SOLOMON. Ah! I'm in the land of darkness here! These people... this country... God! They've bled me dry... Aida? / Aidiyay?

AIDA. I'm here Dad / I can hear you

SOLOMON. Hello? Huh?/ Huh?

AIDA. I can hear you / Dad.

SOLOMON. They are behaving with impunity in this God forsaken airport! Ah! Hello? / Hello?

(Again, in the background there is a faint
sound of children laughing and playing.
SOLOMON *is breathless as he speaks.)*

TSION. Daddy?

SOLOMON. These people are trying to ruin me! Can you hear me / Tsionie?

TSION. *(Taking the phone.)* Daddy, don't worry, I will book you another / ticket yeah?

SOLOMON. No no no no no Tsionie, I will try to get these idiots to refund / me...

TSION. I'll just do it now online Dad / it's fine...

SOLOMON. Online?/ Huh? Tsionie?

TSION. Online / Dad.

SOLOMON. Ah, on the computer!

TSION. It will be in your email.

SOLOMON. No no no no Tsionie... I don't want you to have to pay for these people's incompetence!

TSION. It's fine Dad. I'll book it now. Check your email.

SOLOMON. Huh? Email? Okay... Okay. God bless you Tsionie... God bless you both... is your brother there? Hello? / Tsionie?

TSION. He's outside. / He's

(**SOLOMON** *sounds like he is running.*)

SOLOMON. It's going to cut out Tsionie... Huh? Tsionie? Book, book the ticket, okay?

TSION. Okay Daddy.

(*The phone cuts out.*)

(**YOSI** *comes in with a large pack of paper plates and napkins which he places on the kitchen counter.*)

YOSI. You lot need to stop boying man. Levels yeah, I ain't some likle' yut ya na!

(**YOSI** *goes back out.*)

(**TSION** *starts booking the plane ticket on her phone.*)

TSION. I can book him on one for Wednesday.

AIDA. Is that the earliest?

TSION. The ones for tomorrow and Tuesday are too expensive.

AIDA. Do you want me to pay half?

TSION. Na it's fine, I got it.

AIDA. You sure?

> *(***YOSI*** staggers in carrying a stack of old,
> outdoor plastic chairs. He unstacks the chairs
> and starts to spread them around the space.
> The chairs are weather beaten and covered
> with layers of dust and dirt.)*

YOSI. Yo! I ain't gonna lie these chairs are straight ratchet
bro! *(Noticing the change in* **AIDA** *and* **TSION.***)* What's
wrong with you two?

> *(Beat.)*

AIDA. He's not coming.

YOSI. Why?!

TSION. They cancelled his flight or something innit.

YOSI. What? You lot spoke to him?

TSION. Yeah.

YOSI. Nah, you lot are on some fuckeries! Why didn't you
shout / me?

AIDA. If you wanna chat to him then call him then innit.

YOSI. Bruv, man's on pay as you go, I can't be making no
international calls ya get / me!

AIDA. Broke nigga shit / yeah?

YOSI. / What?!

TSION. *(To* **YOSI.***)* Fam, why you bringing those chairs in
here? Out there in the courtyard, yeah, we'll serve them
out there yeah, not in / here!

YOSI. Oh my dayz! You juss told me to bring them in here!

TSION. Come on Yosh man, we ain't got time, / they're

YOSI. Yo, when's he reaching then?

TSION. Getting him a ticket for Wednesday.

YOSI. This Wednesday?

TSION. Yes, Wednesday. Clean them and take them out by the shade yeah? Let's at least try to make it alright for Mum innit.

YOSI. Thass what I said in the first place fam but you lot don't listen!

> (TSION *rushes back into the kitchen.* YOSI *begrudgingly cleans the chairs before taking them outside.* AIDA *joins him in cleaning the chairs.*)

How can anyone have these chairs in their yard? That's some propa hood shit man.

AIDA. Any piece of furniture Dad found, he'd just drag in ya know!

YOSI. Road side furniture yeah?

AIDA. Used to embarrass the hell out of me and Ife!

YOSI. What? But now you think it's cool coz your vegan friends showed you about upcycling?

AIDA. You're a fool.

YOSI. I'm juss playin'!

> (*Beat.*)

We should all go meet him. Dad. When he gets here on Wednesday, we should go meet him. Man can't touch down and be on his ones ya get me. We need to be there.

AIDA. Look at you!

YOSI. What?

AIDA. All tryin' to be grown and responsible yeah?

YOSI. Yeah, dun know!

AIDA. Yeah?

YOSI. Man a' the house innit!

AIDA. Is it?!

YOSI. Truss.

AIDA. Nah, baby of the house more like!

YOSI. You're a pagan fam!

(Beat.)

AIDA. You propa look like him you know.

YOSI. Ife?

AIDA. Yeah

YOSI. Ah, nah allow that fam!

(Beat.)

Yo, did he ask about me?

AIDA. Dad?

YOSI. Yeah. Did he ask about me?

AIDA. Yeah.

YOSI. What did he say?

AIDA. Just asked if you were around.

YOSI. It's mad innit? Him missing the whole thing.

AIDA. Yosi, let's try to get to that zoot before they get here yeah?

YOSI. Cool. We'll juss take these out now / innt.

(TSION comes back in.)

TSION. We should have some music on in here or something.

YOSI. Tupac innit. Ife tried chattin' to me about Tupac one time when he was here propa high. He said *he* was The Rose That Grew From Concrete fam. I thought that was deep.

> (**YOSI** *connects his phone to the TV speakers and browses through songs.*)

TSION. Bruv man, not that kind of music / they

YOSI. This is Tupac bruv, put some respect on his /name!

AIDA. How about Lethal Bizzle? Ife loved making up routines to Pow!

YOSI. Pow? Rah man, you lot are old!

> (**YOSI** *plays a track*, turns it up loud, bobbing his head, and soon starts dancing and rapping along to it.*)

AIDA. *(Also dancing and rapping along to the lyrics.)* Yes! What? Yo, this was Ife's moves to this!

> (*She dances like Ife. Extravagant, expressive and captivating.*)

TSION. Oi you lot man, we should play some Gospel or / something...

YOSI. *(Even more involved in the song and impressed by* **AIDA**'s *moves.)* Yo brazy moves fam! Braaaaazy! Was that Ife yeah?! What?! / Come on T!

TSION. They're gonna be here any minute / man!

---

* A licence to produce *House of Ife* does not include a performance license for any third-party or copyrighted music. Licensees should create an original composition or use music in the public domain. For further information, please see the Music and Third Party Materials Use Note on page iii.

AIDA. Come on T!

> (**AIDA** *takes* **TSION** *by the hand and dances with her.* **TSION** *reluctantly shuffles to the music but soon starts dancing in her own way.* **AIDA, YOSI** *and* **TSION** *rap and dance together with complete abandon like they are in a rave.*)

> (**MERON** *appears at the door which has been left open. She is dressed in black mourning clothes. A strong woman, steely from her hard-won life as an immigrant. Behind her we can hear the sound of fellow mourners.* **MERON** *shuts the door behind her. She is stunned for a moment as she watches her children dancing, enraptured in the music.*)

MERON. STOP IT! I SAID STOP IT!!

> (**AIDA, TSION** *and* **YOSI** *stop dancing and scramble to turn the music off.*)

What in God's name are you doing?

> (*We hear the sound of more people arriving outside.*)

TSION. Sorry / Mum.

MERON. Look at this place! What have you done?

YOSI. Sorry Mummy.

> (**AIDA** *and* **YOSI** *rush to clean the chairs. The voices of the mourners arriving outside grows.*)

MERON. We've got guests here! Why is the food on the floor?! God help me! They all offered to help but you insisted, instead of coming back to the Church with everyone! And you run here and make this mess? / Eh

AIDA. We were / just...

MERON. Don't disgrace your brother! You hear me? Ah!
My God! They bring us food and you want to put it on
the floor? Eh?

YOSI. I had all / the...

MERON. Quiet! And you were supposed to help them,
instead you are leaping around like this is some... /
some...

AIDA. We were / just...

MERON. On a day like this? Lord help me! These children!

AIDA. Celebrating / him.

> (*There is a knock at the door. Someone calls
> for* MERON.)

MERON. (*To* YOSI.) Take them out some chairs!

> (*More voices of mourners arriving outside.*
> YOSI *manages to open the door after a brief
> struggle. We hear the voices of the mourners
> as they interact with him.* MERON *starts
> picking up the food and arranging the dishes
> on the table.*)

Look at this place! You should have left this to the
ladies of the Church!

> (AIDA *and* TSION *pick up the pots and plates
> off the floor, and put them on the table.*)

AIDA. Ife loved that song Mum.

MERON. Ah! You think this is a house of / dancing?

AIDA. We should celebrate / him!

MERON. Eh? Celebrate? God help me. What celebrate?
Huh? Foolish child!

> (YOSI *comes back in.* AIDA *goes to clean up.*)

(*To* **YOSI**.) Take them out some food. And something to drink. (*To* **TSION**.) You too! They've all been walking in this heat all morning.

AIDA. It was Ife's music.

MERON. Disgraceful!

AIDA. He would have wanted us to dance.

> (**YOSI** *goes to the kitchen and fills up a jug with ice and pours in cartons of juice. Outside we can hear the commotion of more mourners arriving.*)

MERON. You should be mourning. There's nothing to celebrate. Mourn him beating your chests and with wailing. Put the dirt and the earth on your heads, tear your clothes and mourn him. That is how it is supposed to be. That's how our mothers would mourn for us. That is how our brothers and sisters mourn for us. Chant his name, scratch your faces, tear your hair out, throw yourselves on the floor and mourn him. Mourn him for forty days and forty nights. That is how it should be. Mourn him in your hearts forever. He is the first born of this house. Flesh of your flesh. My son. Mourn him like you are mourning for yourselves. Mourn him like we mourn those we love. Honour him. He was your / brother...

TSION. (*Attempting to apologise.*) Mum / we

MERON. Where is your grief for him? Huh? Where is your sorrow?

YOSI. (*Also wanting to apologise.*) Mummy... / I

MERON. I love him like I love each and every one of you. I love him with the last breath in my body. No matter what he became he was my son. My boy...my beautiful boy...my *Ashenafi*...my Ife. Don't disgrace him. Say his name and mourn him.

2.

(Later on that evening.)

(Yosi's bedroom. A claustrophobic space that has accumulated clutter over the years. This used to be Aida's bedroom that she shared with Ife.)

(An old Lion of Juda Ethiopian flag is draped on one of the walls. On one side of the room there is a shelf overflowing with books. Old books, encyclopædias and a box of old Bibles.)

(On the other side of the room is the bunk bed that used to belong to Aida and Ife, now used by Yosi. Aida's bags lay messily open by the bottom bunk along with her paints, rolls of canvases and a half finished painting of Ife.)

(From the sounds offstage we get the sense that the flat is now full of people. Sudden outbursts of wailing can be heard sometimes. The voices in the other room constantly break out into Amharic Spirituals or enraptured prayers. AIDA is clearing up the space to make room for her canvas on the floor so she can paint.)

(Throughout this scene the sounds of prayer, song and voices speaking in tongues from the other room increase and intensify.)

(YOSI enters looking a bit disheveled and wiping sweat off his forehead.)

YOSI. What you doing?

AIDA. Cleaning up.

YOSI. Cleaning up what?

AIDA. These books innit. I dunno why you've got them in here. Put them in the shed or give them to the library man.

YOSI. Yo! Who said you / could

AIDA. I can't work in here with all this / junk

YOSI. Who asked you / to

AIDA. Can you smell it? That smell? The smell of decaying paper. Look. Some of these books got mould on their pages, black mould man, that shit is / dangerous.

YOSI. Fam? Who asked you to clear out the books though?

AIDA. What, you read them or something? Encyclopaedia Britannica, yeah? Ain't you got Google on your / phone?

YOSI. They're asking for you.

AIDA. I'll be there in a / minute.

YOSI. They want to pray for you.

AIDA. Yosi man I need to work. I can't work anywhere else in this / place.

YOSI. They're doing it to T now yeah, that's why they're asking for you / innit.

AIDA. Why they shouting like that?

YOSI. They've clocked you've been movin' booky fam.

AIDA. Shut up man!

YOSI. You been away too long brevs.

AIDA. Fuck sakes man.

> *(A photograph of Solomon falls out of a book that AIDA has in her hands.)*

AIDA. Where did you get this picture of Dad from?

YOSI. Leave it, don't be coming into my space and violating, put it / back.

(YOSI *takes the photograph and the book from* AIDA.)

MERON. *(Offstage.)* YOSIYAS?

YOSI. Don't think you can get away by hiding in here / fam.

MERON. *(Offstage.)* YOSI!

AIDA. I'm not hiding. I need to / work.

YOSI. Nah you are! All hiding in here while man like me is out there ya get me, out there like...like ya get me out there doing the flippin' what du call it...doin' the fuckin' emotional labour and shit ya get me...

AIDA. Emotional labour?

YOSI. You know what I'm saying.

AIDA. Why is that woman shouting like that like no one else lives in this block?!

MERON. *(Offstage.)* YOSI!

YOSI. You should be there with Mum / anyway.

AIDA. I need to put it on there. His transition, I need to work with this / energy

YOSI. What?

AIDA. I need to finish this for Ife. What he was before the... I need to find it on there. Just give me space Yosi, man!

YOSI. Fam, you're sounding nuts!

AIDA. I don't believe in all that superstition there / anyway.

YOSI. Yo, you're going straight to hell juss for sayin that shit / alone!

AIDA. Yosi man, are you gonna let me work? Why you just standing there? What do you want?

YOSI. Fam, it's not that deep – go in there so I can eat and go to bed.

AIDA. Textbooks from the eighties? Why the fuck did he drag these in here?

YOSI. What do you mean working? You're juss dragging it today fam!

AIDA. You know, when I asked him to get me actual revision books for my GCSEs he went on like we asked him to rob a bank or / something!

YOSI. / Don't

AIDA. *How to Win Friends and Influence People*, you read / this?

YOSI. I don't wanna beef with you today fam.

AIDA. What? Roadmen don't read?

MERON. *(Offstage.)* YOSIYAS?

AIDA. He brought all these books but all he ever read was the Bible!

YOSI. So what?

AIDA. These books were just for show and you're holding on to them when they're juss full of dust and / decay!

YOSI. Swear down, you're a dickhead fam.

AIDA. Dad's a showman innit, he wanted to show the community that he was some kind of scholar or something.

YOSI. Dad was a Spiritual leader fam. You should know that.

AIDA. You actually believe that?

YOSI. Yeah, man like him was on some Mandela shit back in the day, ya get me!

AIDA. Joker.

YOSI. Facts bruv! Dad was about bringing the people together innit.

AIDA. He weren't no politician. He juss preached in some road side church out there.

YOSI. Nah, he had to go on the run innit, coz they clocked he had too much power.

AIDA. What? Who told you / that?

YOSI. But man still went back! Still went back for our people den innit. Thass why you have to rate him innit. Man went back to rebuild!

MERON. *(Offstage.)* YOSIYAS?!

AIDA. I get it. You need to create myths to cope with him leaving.

YOSI. Fam why you keep speaking like that? All tryin' trying to act white and / shit!

AIDA. What do you mean act white?

YOSI. Look at you fam! You're from endz but you try talking like some hippie.

AIDA. A hippie?

YOSI. A pagan. A hipster. A fucking yaa ya get me?

AIDA. A fucking yaa? What's a fucking yaa?!

YOSI. You forget who you are bruv!

AIDA. Since when did you start calling your sisters bruv anyway?

YOSI. See what I mean? You're a pagan!

AIDA. That's absurd.

YOSI. See!

AIDA. What?

YOSI. Absurd!

AIDA. It's just my voice.

YOSI. Come on fam don't try it, back in the day you
sounded like any donnie off the endz then all of a
sudden you get into that art school and you come out
sounding / like...like...

  (Enter MERON.)

MERON. *(To YOSI.)* Do you not hear me when I'm calling
you?!

YOSI. I was trying to tell her that the aunties were looking
for / her.

MERON. Eh? You answer me when I call you! You hear?

YOSI. Yes Mummy.

MERON. What are you doing in here? You should both be
out there with them!

YOSI. It's / her

  *(MERON starts rummaging around the
  books, looking for something.)*

MERON. Where are those Bibles? The box with the Bibles?

AIDA. This one?

MERON. They want to pray and quote scripture all night
but they can't even remember to bring their own /
Bibles!

  *(TSION comes in past MERON, looking
  disheveled, sweaty and disoriented, clearly
  the experience she has just had was an
  ordeal.)*

TSION. *(To AIDA.)* The Pastor wants to pray from you /
fam.

YOSI. That's what I'm trying to tell / her!

MERON. *(To AIDA.)* You shouldn't be cooped up in here.

YOSI. / Mummy?

AIDA. I'm working Mum.

MERON. *(To* **AIDA.***)* Ah! What do you mean working? God help me! Working on a day like this?

AIDA. This is for Ife / Mum.

MERON. You can do that in the morning. They have all been asking after you. Go. There is some bread. Go in there and serve them something. Bring them water. There is some juice in the fridge if they want. This heat has been unbearable today.

AIDA. I just need a moment to process.

MERON. What process? They are waiting for you.

YOSI. She's just shook / innit.

AIDA. Shut / up!

MERON. *(To* **YOSI.***)* Stop your bickering. Not today. Do you hear me? *(To* **AIDA.***)* Go in there and show your face. We have to be together with our community today. That is how it should be. It is a sin to work on such a day.

YOSI. She might go in there and start stuttering / again!

MERON. So what you forget your speech, eh? This is nothing to be ashamed of. They were not expecting you to speak. Your father was the one they were expecting. He was the one who should have spoken. Not you. They understand. This is no excuse for hiding in here. They are all here to support us, so go in there and show your face eh? It's the least you can / do.

AIDA. How long are they gonna be in / there?

　　　　(The Pastor suddenly wails in the other room. **MERON** *looks through the gap in the door.)*

MERON. Ah, that young boy! I always thought he was too young to be the leader of our Church! Look at him, eh! He should go back home and see how things are done.

Back home our fathers would be sitting in silence out of respect and when our mothers wailed it was heartfelt, like they were wailing for their own sons, but some of these people... they think they're in an American Church, eh? Forgetting our ways at their age! God help them. Ah look at her! She thinks she's the town crier that woman! I'm sick of her! That woman is... ah how you say... fake! She should cry for her own son, God bless him, that boy is in and out of that mental ward all the time.

YOSI. Who / Ermie?

MERON. She is a gossip!

YOSI. I see Erimie on road all the time innit.

MERON. She keeps asking after your father, like she doesn't know where he is or what he's doing.

YOSI. Shall I tell her to bounce?

TSION. What do you mean tell her to bounce? What do you think this / is?

MERON. Ah! Leave it. Let her wail. She will stop once the Pastor leaves.

TSION. I thought you were friends?

MERON. She thinks I would crumble when your father left but she doesn't know me. I am a soldier.

YOSI. G'wan Mummy! Them lot dun / know!

MERON. Ah, I better get these to them, else they will be here all night. *(To* **AIDA.***)* Come on.

AIDA. I'll be there in a minute Mum.

(**MERON** *exits.*)

YOSI. You alright T?

TSION. There shouldn't be that many people in there man, couldn't even breathe!

YOSI. Them lot are so rago!

TSION. It's like a sauna in there!

YOSI. Some superspreader ting ya get me!

> (**AIDA** *gathers herself and goes to leave the room but can't quite bring herself to cross the threshold.*)

Bruv, do they shout like that in their own homes? That's a violation ya know!

TSION. Innit?

> (*Beat.*)

AIDA. I think I'm having a panic attack!

YOSI. Panic attack? Bruv allow that hippie talk yeah. You're in endz now.

AIDA. Don't be coming at me with your ignorant bars Yosi man. I'm not in the mood.

YOSI. Nah, I'm juss tryin' to show you the realness / fam.

> (**AIDA** *steadies herself and tries to breathe for a moment.*)

TSION. (*To* **YOSI.**) Leave her man. (*To* **AIDA.**) Are you alright?

AIDA. It's Ife... it's like he's haunting me or something... I dunno...

TSION. Shall I come in with you?

AIDA. It's fine.

TSION. You're shaking.

AIDA. I'm fine.

> (**AIDA** *forces herself to leave the room.*)

(YOSI *starts to put the books back on the shelves. He does this carefully, attentive to the books and the order they go in.*)

TSION. What's with the books?

YOSI. Just putting them back.

TSION. Where were they going?

YOSI. Aida wanted to get rid of them innit. Pissing me off / ya know!

TSION. Don't be so hard on her man. She's grieving her twin.

YOSI. Yeah, we're grieving him too fam.

TSION. They were much closer though.

YOSI. Why did she lock him off then?

TSION. She tried bare times. It just didn't work.

(*Beat.*)

YOSI. I can't imagine him without the drugs.

TSION. He was cool ya know. Ife. He had swag.

YOSI. Is it?

TSION. I remember when he left yard. He was sixteen. I remember that day. I snuck out of bed and I see him leaving this room with his bag. And I was juss standing there waving, when he got to the door and came back to hug me. I remember his smell. It was like a mix of CK One and weed smoke. I remember that. It was the last time I remember him being normal.

YOSI. I can't imagine him being normal.

TSION. He was loving. Always loving but he juss always had that side to him innit.

(*Beat.*)

That side to him that didn't fit nowhere, that side that was always restless.

YOSI. I wish I knew him before the drugs.

TSION. Sixteen though!

YOSI. Bare people leave yard at sixteen.

TSION. Nah but he shouldn't have been left alone like that, you get me?

YOSI. He never wanted to be here that's what he told me the last time I saw him, cracked out and fucked up, I don't know if he was dreaming or talking to me but his eyes were half closed and rolling back in his head, I was tryin' to get him to bounce ca he was stinking out the place and he said that he never wanted to be here. Looked me straight in the eye and said that to me fam.

  (Beat.)

TSION. Fuck man...

YOSI. You alright?

TSION. Yeah, I'm just...

YOSI. I know.

TSION. It's just fucked innit?

YOSI. Yeah.

TSION. I wish like... I wish today could..️this could be a celebration of his life instead of all that madness in there.

YOSI. Yeah.

  (Beat.)

I'm starving man.

  *(**TSION** peers through the gap in the door.)*

TSION. They'll be out soon.

(**YOSI** *has a look through the gap in the door.*)

YOSI. She looks numb.

TSION. All them hands on her like rays of the sun!

YOSI. Like branches of a tree fam!

TSION. She looks serene.

YOSI. Look at how Mum's holding her hand.

TSION. What? Wait, they're putting oil on her head? Did they do that to you?

YOSI. Nah fam, they didn't anoint me like that ya know!

TSION. Reaching for her like ~~leapers~~ reaching for Jesus fam!

L lepers

(*Beat.*)

YOSI. It's boilin'.

(**TSION** *moves away from the door.*)

(*The sound of the prayers reach fever pitch.* **TSION** *and* **YOSI** *listen for a moment, looking lost and bewildered.*)

Do you believe him?

TSION. What?

YOSI. That his flight was cancelled?

TSION. Why would I not?

YOSI. Do you think maybe he just didn't wanna come?

TSION. Come on man, of course he wanted to come. He just got delayed that's all.

YOSI. But he's got a new family out there. Maybe he don't wanna deal with us anymore.

(The sounds of prayer and song start dying down in the other room.)

TSION. Nah it's not like that bruv!

*(**YOSI** checks through the gap at the door.)*

YOSI. They're finishing up.

TSION. Finally!

YOSI. Fuckin' starving brevs.

TSION. Mum didn't clock but they've boxed off all the food fam!

YOSI. No!

TSION. Yeah man, they've wiped them trays clean.

YOSI. Ah pissed fam!

TSION. I'll make us something.

YOSI. Nah, these lot need to bounce a-sap, ya get me!

*(**TSION** checks through the gap in the door.)*

TSION. They're almost done now. Wanna go in?

YOSI. Yeah, come.

TSION. Nah, you first bruv!

YOSI. You're still shook innt!

*(**YOSI** opens the door and leaves, **TSION** follows him out.)*

3.

(Early hours of Thursday morning.)

(The air is still humid, a night where it is too hot to sleep. **AIDA** *stumbles in, dancing to music on her headphones. She is tipsy. She has glitter on her face and is still buzzing from her revels.* **TSION** *is sprawled on the floor working on application papers for work placement.* **AIDA** *freezes when* **TSION** *glances at her.)*

TSION. Freezing don't make you invisible ya know!

*(***AIDA*** is still playing this game.)*

You're drunk? You're drunk innit?

*(***AIDA*** giggles.)*

You only laugh like that when you're drunk, you don't think I know?

*(***AIDA*** unplugs her headphones. A UK garage classic blares from her phone*.* **AIDA** *dances joyfully, putting on a show for* **TSION***, who enjoys* **AIDA***'s intoxicated performance.)*

Shhhhh! You're gonna wake them up!

*(***AIDA*** grabs ***TSION****'s hands and pulls her to her feet and dances with her.)*

Ah fam man, I ain't waved like you ya know!

---

* A licence to produce *House of Ife* does not include a performance license for any third-party or copyrighted music. Licensees should create an original composition or use music in the public domain. For further information, please see the Music and Third Party Materials Use Note on page iii.

AIDA. You don't need to be! Look at you!

> *(They dance, trying to out do each other with big, playful Garage dance moves.)*

See? You are wavy as you are T! You don't need nothing else!

TSION. Yeah?

AIDA. You missed a good night!

TSION. What you taken? You high? You're still high innit?

> *(**AIDA** sings lines from a rap song*.)*

> *(**AIDA** takes out two bottles of wine from her bag and places them on the counter.)*

TSION. Fam, what you doin'?

AIDA. I got it!

TSION. What

AIDA. I got it! I'm in the show T!

TSION. She's gonna flip out if she sees that ya know!

AIDA. Screw top. See? I thought ahead innit. You want some?

TSION. Fam, you know there ain't no alcohol allowed in this house.

AIDA. Come on T! We have to celebrate!

> *(**AIDA** pours two glasses of wine and gives one to **TSION.** They clink glasses. **AIDA** takes a big swig.)*

---

* A licence to produce *House of Ife* does not include a performance license for any third-party or copyrighted music. Licensees should create an original composition or use music in the public domain. For further information, please see the Music and Third Party Materials Use Note on page iii.

TSION. I'm happy for you.

AIDA. Whitechapel Gallery!

TSION. About time. You're propa talented innit fam!

> (**AIDA** *pours herself another glass.*)

AIDA. I fuckin' miss London man!

> (*Beat.*)

I miss it all the time.

TSION. Move back then. I dunno why you even bounced in the first place!

AIDA. Love innit.

TSION. Nah. You moved thirsty!

AIDA. I moved for love!

TSION. You moved bare reckless fam!

AIDA. All for love!

TSION. And how did that work out then?

AIDA. Love is a battle. Love is a war. Love is growing up, T!

TSION. What?!

AIDA. Nah, I read that somewhere. Baldwin I think.

TSION. You're just too proud to move back innit?

AIDA. Anyway, what's going on with yoooooou T?

TSION. What?

AIDA. Come on T, what? You didn't think I see the way you were preeing that donnie / at Church?

TSION. Why you always talk so hood when you're drunk?

AIDA. Nah, don't change the subject T! What? Is that your ting / yeah?

TSION. Shhhhhhh!

AIDA. Ahhhhh! You lot were moving bait! You think I didn't clock?

TSION. They're all / sleeping!

AIDA. G'wan T! What is that your side-piece or something? What happed to my man? What's his name / ...?

TSION. Who, Sammy?

AIDA. Yeah, what happed to him?

TSION. Nah, he's a wasteman / fam.

AIDA. What? Is that how you're moving T?

TSION. He's juss not on anything / innit.

AIDA. Keepin' dem breddas on smash, yeah?

TSION. *(Amused.)* You're a / fool!

AIDA. When you linking this new donnie then?

TSION. He tried moving to me with some dead bars ya know!

AIDA. Swear down?

TSION. Yeah, sending me poems and shit! Moist bredda!

AIDA. I don't blame him. I'd be sending you poems too T!

TSION. Fam! / You're

AIDA. Oi, I love you, you know that yeah don't you? I love you like my heart is about to explode T...to the moon and back... I love you like that innit...how much do you love me?

TSION. Aida man you're / wasted.

AIDA. You do love me though don't you T?

TSION. You're gonna wake the whole house up / fam!

AIDA. I'm not...

(**AIDA** *leaps to her feet and does an extravagant balletic movement.*)

See! I'm not drunk!

(*As* **AIDA** *dances around the room, she trips over some luggage by the wall. A large suitcase wrapped in cellophane and a couple of half open bags that contain objects and fabrics wrapped in plastic bags and Amharic newspapers.*)

(*Beat.*)

He arrived okay?

TSION. Yeah. He was asking after you fam. Thought you were gonna be there to pick him up innit.

AIDA. Where is he?

TSION. In there with Yosh.

AIDA. He's not staying in Tottenham?

TSION. Said he wants to be near us innit.

AIDA. Is he alright?

TSION. He's in a state. He cried himself to sleep. I could hear him through the walls.

AIDA. How does he look? Has he changed?

TSION. He looks devastated fam. Fragile innit. It's like the first time I saw him and clocked that he's actually an old man. Came all this way and he's sleeping on the bottom bunk in there like a kid. I felt bad, he looked embarrassed innit, but there was nowhere else.

(*Beat.*)

You can sleep with me fam.

AIDA. I ain't seen him in years ya know. Can't even remember the last time I…

TSION. He's proper broken up by all this. Mum barely said a few words to him.

(*Beat.*)

I wish she'd not deep it though. He feels bad enough as it is.

AIDA. He left her for another woman, what do you expect?

TSION. Nah I get / that

AIDA. Married her when he was still married to Mum.

TSION. People break up. People get divorced. It's normal.

AIDA. Nah but, that's like bigamy innit? That shit's a crime ya know.

TSION. Get some sleep, you're drunk.

AIDA. She's my age isn't she? His wife? My age with four kids! Huh! Man wasted no time breeding her up boy!

TSION. Why you talkin' like this?

AIDA. It's true though innit? He replaced us quick!

TSION. As long as he's happy, then, that's all that matters ya get me.

AIDA. Yeah I know / but

TSION. You should have gone with Yosh to pick him up. He was upset that you weren't there.

AIDA. He's not a kid. He don't need me to pick him up. Anyway Yosi was there / so

TSION. Nah, but you're his favourite. You're still his favourite fam.

AIDA. Four kids. It's crazy innit? Four kids at his age?! I dunno what he was / thinking!

TSION. Fam, you're shouting.

AIDA. It pisses me off. When people do that. Like, have all them extra kids when they can't even look after the ones they already have!

TSION. We don't need him / to

AIDA. He can't even look after himself. Only time he calls is to ask for money. That's it. Never coz he's wondering how I am, it's always about money / it's

TSION. He's been building that house for us fam.

AIDA. Come on T man, you just paid for his plane ticket!

TSION. It's fine. He's struggling isn't he? I don't mind helping.

    (Beat.)

Said he keeps calling you but you never answer. You need to make an effort with him fam. It's like you've locked him off. You've juss been blanking him since you left. You ain't made an effort with him for years fam. It's not always about money. Sometimes it's just about answering and seeing how he is, innit. You can't always be assuming he wants money from you. At least he calls you. He don't really call me and Yosh you know. When he does, he's always asking about you.

    (Beat.)

AIDA. Ah... T man, I'm sorry.

TSION. It's fine.

    (Silence.)

    *(**TSION** goes back to working on her applications. **AIDA** pours herself another glass. She starts drinking then stops, suddenly needing to speak...)*

AIDA. I can't paint. I ain't been able to paint properly. Every time I try, it's him that comes out. Just portraits of him. I can't get away from it. It's like he's haunting me T.

TSION. Fam, you should chat to someone about this / ya know.

AIDA. *(Placing her hand on her chest.)* He's like right here. I feel him right here. Ever since I saw him in the mortuary he's always been here, it's like he's possessed me or something. I try but I can't seem to paint anything else T.

I couldn't even speak for him when I got up there the other day. I was just numb. It was like I was in that box with him.

> *(Beat.)*

We should have never let him get like that T. We all just gave up on / him.

TSION. I don't want to chat about this.

AIDA. We have to be accountable T.

TSION. Accountable?

AIDA. Yeah, we all have to be accountable / about what

TSION. Fam, this ain't one of your podcasts yeah so allow it with all the woke shit.

> (**TSION** *gathers her things and heads out of the room.*)

TSION. I'm gong to bed.

AIDA. I'm sorry. I'm just / a bit

TSION. There's some aspirins in that top drawer.

AIDA. T man, I'm sorry. But / we

TSION. It's fine. I just... I just don't wanna chat about all that right now.

(TSION *exits.*)

(AIDA *pours herself another drink and downs it. She pours another one and continues drinking.*)

4.

(Later that morning.)

*(**YOSI** and **SOLOMON** sit together on the couch. **YOSI** tinkers on a keyboard, trying to write a song. **SOLOMON** watches him amused. **YOSI** has an earphone in one ear and is wearing a bright coloured t-shirt over his work uniform. Yosi's t-shirt has Amharic writing on it.)*

SOLOMON. Ohhhhhh wee ohhh wee ohhh wee ohhh wee!!! Eh? It is hotter than the desert today isn't it son?

YOSI. They said it's gonna be another scorcher today.

SOLOMON. Back home there is always a breeze you know? A cool, cool breeze no matter how hot it gets. God's air-conditioning is always on down there son, not like here, not like this God forsaken country / it never

YOSI. Yeah, it's been propa hot this year.

SOLOMON. Never used to get like this. London I mean. You could breathe in the summer back then...

YOSI. They reckon it's gonna be the hottest summer on record.

SOLOMON. Good Lord have mercy. We are burning up God's planet!

YOSI. Burning it up?

SOLOMON. Making ungodly summers like this.

YOSI. What? You're Greta Thunburg now yeah?

SOLOMON. Vanity of vanities, says the Preacher, vanity of vanities!

YOSI. Thought you said it was all a hoax?

SOLOMON. All is vanity.

YOSI. What?

SOLOMON. The farm land in Ethiopia is not producing any harvest and London feels like it's on fire, I'm telling you son we have offended the Almighty with our vanity!

YOSI. Do you reckon God would move petty like that though?

SOLOMON. You're not listening!

> (**YOSI** *sings a few lines from a song by an artist like Kendrick Lamar*.*)

SOLOMON. Ah! Excuse me?!

YOSI. It's a song. Kendrick innit. He's a spiritual lyricist. I reckon you'd like / him.

SOLOMON. FOOKERAH!

YOSI. What?

SOLOMON. That's what we call it back home. Fookerah. This rapping things. We were rapping before these even people knew how to read or write!

YOSI. Rah! Is it?!

SOLOMON. But our fookerah was always about our people and our land and our heroes!

YOSI. Jheeeeeeeze!

SOLOMON. Ah! But our land is burning up and we are fighting each other. We have nothing to *mehfoker* about anymore son.

YOSI. Nah, next climate march ting, I'm reachin', truss!

SOLOMON. Are you reading your Bible son?

---

* A licence to produce *House of Ife* does not include a performance license for any third-party or copyrighted music. Licensees should create an original composition or use music in the public domain. For further information, please see the Music and Third Party Materials Use Note on page iii.

YOSI. Sometimes, when I'm barrin' innit.

SOLOMON. "Do not call conspiracy all that this people calls conspiracy, and do not fear what they fear, nor be in dread." Which one is that one?

YOSI. Huh?

SOLOMON. Isaiah 8:12 son, read your Bible. Contemplate His Word instead of this rapping thing.

YOSI. Dad man, you clocked it time ago! They don't want us to be like, what du call it...industrialised innit! Coz, like they've already made their peas and built their machines and factories and done polluting the air and rinsing the out the land, but they don't want that for Africa, ya get me? They want Africans to stay broke innit? Keep us broke so they always have power over us! These lot are on some recolonising ting, innit!

SOLOMON. You are wrong son. We were never colonised. Your forefathers defeated the Europeans not once but twice! You should know your history! Ethiopia has always been free. Always.

YOSI. Amen!

SOLOMON. And industrialisation is not the answer! The only / thing

YOSI. Nah obviously I'm not saying like you said exactly them words / but you

SOLOMON. The only thing that Africa needs right now, more than ever son, is the Word of God! You understand what I'm saying to you?

YOSI. Nah, broke people innit. Broke niggas always need religion ya get me!

SOLOMON. Why you start to speak like this / eh?

YOSI. Sorry.

SOLOMON. You speak like this because of this nonsense you are listening to, eh?

YOSI. It's not nonsense Dad, you should hear my new / stuff.

SOLOMON. You are not *a nigga* you are an Ethiopian, remember that.

YOSI. Nah that depends innit / like

SOLOMON. We have a country, we have a history son, there are no niggers in Ethiopia. There are no niggers in Africa!

YOSI. Brrrraaaappppp!! I rate that ya know!

SOLOMON. Leave that word to people here who seem to need it, but that word is not for us, not for you / and me.

YOSI. No niggers in Ethiopia! No niggers in Africa! That's a bar ya know. That's greazy! I might have to borrow dat still!

SOLOMON. You can make your music for Christ, son.

YOSI. Nah, allow me Dad man.

SOLOMON. There are many young people like you in our Church who would listen if you made songs for / Him.

YOSI. Gospel rap, what in / Amharic?!

SOLOMON. We are building a House of God, son.

YOSI. I'm not on no Gospel rap / ting.

SOLOMON. Ah! Don't shackle yourself son, see...when the Word is within you...

> (**SOLOMON** *proceeds to hammer out a discordant tune and starts singing a half improvised Gospel song.* **YOSI** *is tickled, and can't hold back his laughter at* **SOLOMON***'s eccentric performance.*)

> (*Relishing the attention from* **YOSI** *and being even bigger with his performance.*) I'm a warrior for Christ son! Listen!

YOSI. Dad man, you're gonna shatter the windows with that off-key / tune man!

SOLOMON. Ah, let the Spirit move you / boy!

YOSI. Nah music ain't your ting, you need to stick to the preaching / Dad!

SOLOMON. Listen... Eh! ...Listen... Feel the Spirit... Yes Lord! ...

> (**SOLOMON** *struggles to find the lyrics of the Spiritual he is half improvising and belting out.* **YOSI** *steps in and playfully freestyles some rap lyrics.* **SOLOMON** *loves it and enthusiastically tries to accompany* **YOSI** *by hammering down on the keys.* **YOSI** *relishes this attention from* **SOLOMON.** *The music soon becomes chaotic and joyous but quickly falls apart. Their laughter fills the room.)*

> (**AIDA** *enters. She is carrying her painting in a large canvas holder.)*

Aida...? Aidiyay...?

AIDA. Dad...

> (**SOLOMON** *rushes over and hugs her.)*

SOLOMON. Aida! My girl... Ah, I missed you... I've missed you so much! Ahhh Aidiyay! Let me look at you... ah... you've lost weight and your eyes.. your eyes.. they're bigger.. ah, what's all this eh? You've become skinny! Have you been eating properly? You are a fashion model now or what, eh?

AIDA. Dad, are you alright? I was / just

SOLOMON. They told me you were out when I got here. I thought I'd see you at the airport. I stayed up waiting for you. Ah Aida, it is so good to see you! If it weren't for your brother here, I'd have been lost like the first time I came here! But he's a good boy, your brother, we took the Piccadilly, I didn't want him to waste his money on the taxi, he brought me home in one piece.

AIDA. It's good to see you Dad. I've been meaning to call / and

SOLOMON. No, no, no it's fine Aida! I'm just, my heart! Ah, my heart is better now that I've seen you! Come here!

(SOLOMON *hugs* AIDA *again.*)

Praise God. Praise God that we are under one roof again daughter!

(*Beat.*)

AIDA. It's really heartbreaking what's been going on over there Dad. I've been thinking about / you and

SOLOMON. Ah, war is hell isn't it... People of the same blood turning against each other, but I am doing what I can to help. I am fighting to save lives in His name.

AIDA. I was worried about you and / your

SOLOMON. No, no, no, no, don't worry about me. I am doing God's work. We will one day look beyond what divides us and come together, one family in the House of God. It has already been written "Princes shall come out of Egypt; and / Ethiopia shall soon stretch out her hands onto God."

YOSI. *Ethiopia shall soon stretch out her hands onto God!* Brrrrraaaaaapp!!!

(*Beat.*)

SOLOMON. We shouldn't be strangers like this eh? Not you and I, Aida.

AIDA. I will be there next summer.

SOLOMON. Ah! You will visit us?

AIDA. Mum was saying I can use part of the new house out there as a studio.

SOLOMON. Your art! You are still making your art, huh? That painting you gave me when you were just a little girl, Jesus as he actually was you said, an African! You were right, it says so in the Bible; "Hair like wool, feet like burned brass."

AIDA. You've still got it?

SOLOMON. I knew you were gifted even then. When you come you should make us more art like that painting you made. It is on our wall. Above the pulpit as I preach. The people love it. They are always asking me about it.

YOSI. What? Her painting?

SOLOMON. Ah! She's a great artist, your sister!

AIDA. Ah nah Dad / man...

SOLOMON. You are! You must always know that!

(YOSI *puts his other earphone in his ear.*)

AIDA. Thanks Dad...

(*Beat.*)

How is your family?

SOLOMON. Huh?

AIDA. How are your kids doing out / there?

SOLOMON. Wait...wait there...

(**SOLOMON** *goes to his pile of luggage and retrieves a present wrapped in an Amharic newspaper, which he gives to* **AIDA**.*)

AIDA. What's this?

SOLOMON. It's for you.

AIDA. You didn't need to bring me anything.

SOLOMON. Open it. See what you think!

> (**AIDA** *opens the the package and sees that it is a cheap looking bright coloured t-shirt with Amharic writing on it like the one* **YOSI** *is wearing.)*

Try it... See how it suits your brother? One of the best young tailors in Addis made it for us. He is from our Church. Our Church is growing now Aida, that's why we have to build. He made for you. Feel the fabric... see it's quality... see? Not like the rubbish they sell here. Real quality Aida. Go on. Try it on...

> (**AIDA** *does not want to try it on.)*

YOSI. Yo Dad, next time yeah, get me a ring with The Lion of Juda on it. You know like the one Haile Selassie I used to wear? You know he gave that ring to Bob / Marley!

SOLOMON. Son, I will bring it to you in gold next / time! *(To* **AIDA**.) Go on, try it, see what it says.

AIDA. Is Mum / here?

SOLOMON. Ah, she rushed off to Church early this morning.

AIDA. You should have come here sooner Dad, Mum's had to deal with everything on her own.

YOSI. What do you mean? Me and T been here / fam!

SOLOMON. These people Aida! They cancel the plane and I nearly get into a fight at the airport. I don't know what came over me but I was ready to send them to hell with my fists!

AIDA. I've got a meeting / Dad.

SOLOMON. Try it on. The t-shirt. Go on. Try it on. See if it fits.

AIDA. I've got to run / I'm

SOLOMON. Ah! Read it! You have forgotten our language daughter. You have forgotten? I can understand with him, but you were born there, you should never forget your own language!

>   *(Beat.)*

Me-da-ni you know what it / means?

YOSI. Greetings innit?

SOLOMON. No! This boy! You don't listen do you?

>   *(**YOSI** starts sounding out the letters in Amharic in a futile effort to read the language.)*

Salvation! It means Salvation! You don't even speak it now do you? I always tried to speak to you in our language but you forget / eh?

YOSI. Salvation?

SOLOMON. *Addis Medani Alum.* It's the name of our Church Aida! Try it on! See how it fits.

AIDA. Dad, I'm already running late / I

YOSI. What? You went out and got licked again?

AIDA. Shut up Yosi man!

YOSI. Got twist up / yeah?

SOLOMON. *(Clipping **YOSI** around the head.)* She is your elder, son. Show some respect.

YOSI. Ah, Dad man!

AIDA. Can we talk later Dad?

>   *(**YOSI** turns on his video game.)*

SOLOMON. Wait, show me! Your painting is in here? Show me I want to see your great art! Your brother and sister tell me you are always painting. Show me something. I want to see, eh?

(**AIDA** *reluctantly takes her painting out of the canvas holder. It is the painting of Ife from earlier which she has been working on. At the sight of this painting* **SOLOMON** *is winded. He covers his face, he is full of grief.* **YOSI** *stops his game and looks at his father.* **AIDA** *packs the painting away again.*)

AIDA. Sorry Dad, I...We can talk later...

(**AIDA** *hurries out.*)

SOLOMON. My child, my dear, dear child.

(**YOSI** *has returned to his video game. He is speaking to a player online.*)

YOSI. Is that your mum? Why don't you run to her like last time you pussy!

SOLOMON. *(To* YOSI.*)* Ah! Turn that thing off! You need to focus on your education instead of this nonsense.

YOSI. I don't care where you are bruv! We're drillers out here in London, ya see meh!

SOLOMON. Son are you / listening?

YOSI. Shut up! What? Skengman is coming for / you!

SOLOMON. You are not a child anymore, turn that thing / off!

YOSI. Yeah run you American / dickhead!

SOLOMON. Eh? Are you listening!?

YOSI. *(Mouthing "One-sec-let-me-just-finish-this-game" to* SOLOMON, *then back to the game.*) Go run to your mum you bumba hol'! / Watch this!

SOLOMON. Yosiyas! I'm not going to ask you / again!

YOSI. *(Mouthing again "One-sec-Dad", then –.)* Watch me buss up your rass clat! Yeah what? Me? London innit! *(Clearly winning.)* What? See? Nah, you're not that guy! You're not that guy! Watch... Watch / this ⸺

> *(**SOLOMON** abruptly unplugs the screen.)*

Ah Dad! Come on man! I was just about to merc him!!

SOLOMON. What are you doing, eh?

YOSI. It's a game Dad! It's just a game innit!

SOLOMON. You speak like this in this house, eh? I leave you as the man of the house and you are playing games and speaking like this instead of thinking about your future?

YOSI. It's about strategy. It's strategy training innit it's, it's educational, it's not a game like, it's not for kids it's a different kind / of game

SOLOMON. Strategy for what?

YOSI. How to lead a team and be tactical and that innit.

> *(**YOSI** takes off his bright t-shirt, revealing the Sainsbury's uniform he is wearing underneath.)*

SOLOMON. Instead of wasting time with these idiots on the internet you should be reading your books and studying day and night son. You think these people are going to let you play games once you are out there in the world? You should be chewing those books thinking about your future, not playing games like a child!

> *(**SOLOMON** goes to open the windows.)*

YOSI. Those windows don't open properly.

SOLOMON. You should be revising and preparing to return to school. Don't throw away the opportunity these people give you like your brother did! Make something of your life!

YOSI. Nah, / obviously

SOLOMON. If you carry on like this, playing this nonsense thing, there will be no space in here for your books! Think. Think carefully about your future.

YOSI. Nah I will, I have to cut... I have to go now Dad...my shift is starting soon / innit.

SOLOMON. Choose your books instead of this thing okay? Remember if they work once you have to work ten, twenty times harder, that's how you show them yes?

YOSI. Yes Dad.

SOLOMON. Ah! What is this posture, eh? Stand up straight. You are a Child of God. Don't you forget that you hear me?

YOSI. Yeah I hear you Dad.

SOLOMON. Ah! And comb your hair!

YOSI. Ah, Dad man, allow me.

SOLOMON. Go on then.

YOSI. *(Not knowing what to do around* **SOLOMON.***)* See you later Dad...

SOLOMON. God bless you son.

    (Beat.)

Go before you miss your shift. Straight!

    *(***YOSI*** *exits.)*

    *(***SOLOMON*** *is alone in the space. He is uncomfortable being here. He looks around as though discovering the space again. Struggling with memories of the years spent here, memories that seep through the walls*

*and seem to be all around him. He starts
unpacking but he is uneasy and distracted.
He gazes out the window. He is overwhelmed
with loss and longing.)*

5.

(Later that afternoon. The sun is high and the air is heavy with heat.)

*(**MERON** and **SOLOMON** are in the small concrete front yard which also serves as Meron's makeshift garden of potted plants. **MERON** waters and tends to her plants.)*

(Beat.)

MERON. You gave up on him.

SOLOMON. Don't say that! Please don't say that. We have to leave it to God now.

MERON. I read somewhere that when children get addicted like that it is because they are hurt somewhere inside. It's not a choice. It is not because they choose the drugs, it is their way of healing from what has hurt them.

SOLOMON. What healing? Look what he did to himself?

MERON. You couldn't even be here to bury him.

MERON. These past eight years he was always asking about you.

SOLOMON. I was always thinking about him.

MERON. You should have taken him with you when you left.

SOLOMON. The house wasn't finished.

MERON. Even if the house wasn't finished, you should have listened when I asked.

(Beat.)

You were always so hard on him.

SOLOMON. I wanted to do right by him. I was hard on him
because he needed me to be. It was my responsibility as
his father to raise him to be a man. That softness...That
darkness in him / was

MERON. You drove him away from me.

SOLOMON. I worked until my back broke, worked every
day that God sent to make sure there was food in his
belly and clothes on his back. I didn't humiliate myself
all these years in this damn country, cleaning toilets
when I should have been serving God for him to end
up the way he did! I never gave up on him. There was
always a hope in my heart – that God would show us
His mercy and bring the boy back to us. I never gave
up. As God is / my witness

MERON. I don't want to hear this anymore.

(*Beat.*)

(**MERON** *returns to tending her plants.*)

(**SOLOMON** *is restless. He paces, uneasy and
on edge.*)

MERON. When you get back to Addis, make sure you give
the keys to the agents there. They haven't been able
to get in. There are some tenants they want to show
around.

(*Beat.*)

SOLOMON. Is this what it all comes down to in the end?
Slabs of stone on my boy lost in a strange land forever...

(*Beat.*)

Was it expensive?

MERON. What?

SOLOMON. Getting his photo on there?

MERON. It was the best I could afford. The Church helped. I don't know what I would have done without them.

SOLOMON. That picture you put on the gravestone... it's... wasn't there another picture you could have chosen?

MERON. I want to remember him as he was.

SOLOMON. You should have chosen a better picture. That picture / it's...

MERON. He was like that for most of his adult life. I'm not going to put a picture of a child on there am I?

SOLOMON. It would have been better just to have his name on there. More dignified.

MERON. You're still ashamed of him aren't you? Even / now...

SOLOMON. No, it's not that, it's just... I want him to look his best I...

MERON. That was his best. He was happy the day that picture was taken.

(*Silence.*)

MERON. Being here is what killed him.

SOLOMON. Ah! There's plenty of drugs in Ethiopia. Plenty of hopeless kids hooked on drugs back there. It was always in him. That's what he was drawn to. The boy had his demons and they would have been with him anywhere he went.

MERON. We should have tried.

SOLOMON. Stop saying that to me Meron.

(*Beat.*)

SOLOMON. I never slept did I? Traipsed across the city to look for him every time he got lost. Sat in the police station waiting for him every time he got arrested.

Fought with him every morning to get him to school.
Begged his teachers to give him a chance when they
wanted to expel him...pleaded with him to give life a
chance even when he would disrespect me...his father...
I did try... I begged him until I had no more tears left. I
couldn't reach him...it was like he wanted to be lost to
me. The more I tried the more he hated me for it. God
knows I tried.

> (**SOLOMON** *is overcome with grief, he*
> *struggles to stop himself from weeping.*
> *Silence.*)

MERON. I used to have this dream...this nightmare...this
reoccurring nightmare before we came to this country...
I would keep having this nightmare of burying him.
Seeing him disappear into the earth. Into the *lisho*,
the concrete that they would pour over his coffin and
I would beat the earth trying to get it to open back up.
Claw at the earth and the concrete trying to get my Ife
back and I would keep digging...digging with my bare
hands but the more I dug the further away the earth
would take him from me and I'd wake up drenched and
sobbing...and I'd sit by his bed watching him until the
sun came up.

> (*Beat.*)

SOLOMON. You never told me about that.

MERON. I was ashamed of having such things in my head.

SOLOMON. You should have told me.

MERON. I was scared that even uttering a word of it might
tempt fate so I kept it buried until it stopped...

SOLOMON. We should have prayed from that day. Day and
night we should have prayed.

MERON. I did. Day and night I did.

But God didn't listen.

> (*MERON* is overcome with her grief.
> *SOLOMON* moves towards *MERON*. *MERON*
> does not know how to respond.)

SOLOMON. Faith...

MERON. What?

SOLOMON. We can't lose faith...

> (*Silence.*)

SOLOMON. Please?

MERON. What?

SOLOMON. I've missed this...

MERON. Solomon...

SOLOMON. I've missed us...

> (*SOLOMON* suddenly embraces *MERON*. He
> does not let go. She holds him. Both fierce
> and desperate in their embrace. They hold
> each other like two people trying to save each
> other from drowning. Something about their
> physical contact and their grief ignites a
> carnal desire, they want to lose themselves in
> each other.)

> (*SOLOMON* and *MERON* kiss passionately.
> *AIDA* appears and sees them.)

6.

(A sweltering late afternoon, the following day. **SOLOMON** *and* **TSION** *are at an outdoor table of a local coffee shop that has recently been transformed into an upmarket café.* **SOLOMON** *has a well-worn leather document holder with him.* **TSION** *browses her phone.* **SOLOMON** *studies the space around him, fanning himself, impressed by what he sees.)*

SOLOMON. Ah, these people! They know how to live, eh? Look at this place! They have improved it, eh? It used to be like Mogadishu around here!

TSION. You can't say that Dad!

SOLOMON. Huh?

TSION. You can't say things like / that.

SOLOMON. Ah, where is she?

TSION. She'll be here.

SOLOMON. Always like this. Never answers! Call her. We should call her / again...

*(*YOSI *comes out of the café, haphazardly carrying a tray of iced coffees to the table.)*

YOSI. Fuckin' Karen man! I swear down! Pissing / me off!

SOLOMON. Eh? Wash this obscene talk from your mouth son!

YOSI. Tryin' to move to man like I'm some dickhead, / ya know!

SOLOMON. Ah! What is wrong with you / son?

YOSI. Tried gripsing me up/ innit!

SOLOMON. Son, sit / down!

YOSI. Grabbing me up ya know! Do I look like a victim fam?!

TSION. Wait, / what?

YOSI. I ain't no victim, ya / get me!

SOLOMON. Son please.

TSION. What? Some Karen gripsed you / up?

SOLOMON. Karen?

YOSI. Yeah Karen, innit!

SOLOMON. Who the hell is Karen?

YOSI. Some pagan / innit!

SOLOMON. Cool down son, just.. just cool / down

YOSI. Tried calling man belligerent / fam!

TSION. Why? What did you / do?

YOSI. What? What do you mean? Ordering coffee / innit!

SOLOMON. *(To* YOSI.*)* You are a child of God. A child of God. You have no business with this Karen! You understand me son?

>   *(Beat.)*

Ah! Where's your sister?

YOSI. *(Kissing his teeth.)* I shoulda told her to go back to fuckin' Bitchfield or wherever the fuck she comes from, ya get me!

>   *(*SOLOMON *clips* YOSI *around the head.)*

Awww Dad man! What was that for?!

SOLOMON. Why do you keep speaking like this, eh?

TSION. He thinks he is a roadman / innit

SOLOMON. What roadman? I didn't raise you to speak like this!

YOSI. Nah I was / just

(*YOSI kisses his teeth.*)

(*TSION calls AIDA but there is no answer.*)

What is it Dad? What did you want to chat about anyway?

SOLOMON. I wanted your sister to be here first.

YOSI. Are you having another baby?

SOLOMON. No.

YOSI. You moving back to London?

SOLOMON. No son.

YOSI. What is it then?

(*Beat.*)

SOLOMON. She's not picking up?

TSION. Keeps going to voicemail.

YOSI. We're here innit Dad, you can talk to us.

(*Beat.*)

It's always about her man. She's probably in some warehouse somewhere painting tyres with her hippie friends.

SOLOMON. Your sister is an artist son. You should be proud of her.

YOSI. Painted tyres ain't art ya get me.

SOLOMON. You have to support each other. With the three of you supporting each other, you can do anything. Nothing will stand in your way if the three of you work together. See, your sister graduated from one of the finest Art schools in the country! You have to follow in her footsteps and be successful like her.

YOSI. Dad man, she's ain't successful, she's broke.

SOLOMON. It's not always about money son. It's about what you do!

YOSI. What do I do then?

    (Beat.)

SOLOMON. Huh?

YOSI. Me. What do I do?

SOLOMON. This rapping thing but it is not going to get you anywhere. You have to concentrate on your studies.

TSION. Dad, that's not fair.

YOSI. See what I mean. It's always about her.

SOLOMON. No son, I am only saying that because you have potential. You have to fulfill that potential. You should be studying to go to Oxford or Cambridge!

YOSI. What I do *is* art though / Dad.

SOLOMON. If I came from a rural village in Ethiopia where I had to study with a kerosene lamp in dark, imagine what you can do, eh? Both of you. You can be great people. Eh! If I came here at your age / I would be multimillionaire by now!

TSION & YOSI. I would be multimillionaire by now!

    (Beat.)

TSION. How come you never ask?

SOLOMON. What do you want me to ask you?

TSION. About our lives, about what we do, about our friends – you know, the normal things parents / ask.

YOSI. You should juss need to shout us more / innit

SOLOMON. You are busy.

YOSI. Nah, what it / is yeah

SOLOMON. You have busy lives here. / I...

TSION. Just because you divorced Mum don't mean you have to go on like you've divorced us as / well.

YOSI. Dad? / Dad...

SOLOMON. No Tsionie! Why do you say this? You are my / priority.

TSION. Your / priority?

SOLOMON. You. My children. You two and your sister are always my / priority.

TSION. See, you're not even listening.

YOSI. Nah, she's juss sayin' you should check for us and that / innit.

SOLOMON. I brought you here didn't I?

TSION. Here?

SOLOMON. To this country. I brought you to this country didn't I?

TSION. I was born here.

SOLOMON. You two were born here, yes, but I came here because I wanted you all to have a better life.

TSION. Dad, you just need to be a bit more interested in us. I don't see you for years and you still haven't asked about what I'm doing!

SOLOMON. You're working.

TSION. Yes, but you don't even ask what I do!

SOLOMON. You're a teacher.

TSION. What do I teach?

SOLOMON. Tsionie, I am so proud of you, you know that don't / you?

TSION. Just answer the question.

SOLOMON. What do you want me to / say?

TSION. I'm training to be a primary school teacher, Dad. I'm not a teacher yet, you should at least know / that.

SOLOMON. I know that, of course I know that / Tsionie.

YOSI. Yo Dad, you know I'm doing English Lit in / college?

SOLOMON. *(Dismissive.)* Son, please. *(To* **TSION.***)* Where is all this coming from, eh?

YOSI. *(To* **SOLOMON.***)* You being off-grid / innit.

TSION. You're always going on about education and all that, but where were you when I graduated? It's like you didn't have a clue or didn't even / care!

YOSI. Yo Dad, I've been writing / innit

SOLOMON. I'm in the dirt out there Tsionie, out there on the frontline doing God's work, I don't have the luxury of being like these Western / parents.

TSION. It's got nothing to do with being / "Western"

SOLOMON. You both belong here so I don't blame / you.

TSION. It's complicated.

SOLOMON. I know. / I...

TSION. I mean belonging and all that.

SOLOMON. Ah, you were born here. This is your country, daughter. You should thank God and embrace it.

TSION. But, I've never felt the kind of belonging I felt that one time we went back. It was mad. Like... I felt like I was related to all those strangers on the streets or something... and like they looked at me different. Like everyone looked at me different over there... the way they looked at me... like they knew me or something... I dunno... I can't explain it...

SOLOMON. Poverty makes them look at you like that.

TSION. It was like they looked at me like I was home...

SOLOMON. They look at you like that because they want something from you. Hunger does that to people.

TSION. No. It was soft. There was a softness in their eyes.

SOLOMON. Beggars gaze.

TSION. You don't get / it.

SOLOMON. They used to look at me like that as well. "Diaspora"! They are saying when my back is turned, and laughing at me!

TSION. You don't get it / Dad.

SOLOMON. What do you want me to / say?

YOSI. Just call Dad, all you have to do is just call / innit.

SOLOMON. You can call too.

TSION. Dad man, why you gettin' like / that?

SOLOMON. You both should call, you have brothers and sisters over there too, you / know.

TSION. Half.

SOLOMON. They ask for you.

YOSI. Is it?

TSION. Half brothers and sisters.

SOLOMON. They ask for their big brother and sisters.

TSION. We ain't even met / them.

SOLOMON. No harm in sending them some sweets or some toys or something once in a while.

TSION. Send them / stuff?

YOSI. Okay / cool.

SOLOMON. Just small tokens, that's all they need, just so that they know you are also thinking of them like they are thinking of you.

TSION. See what I mean? Now you got all these kids out there it's like you've forgotten about us.

SOLOMON. Do you not see what has been happening to our country? I'm doing God's work there Tsionie. There, where poverty and hunger roams the streets. You should see them Tsionie, whole families, mothers younger than you begging for bread with their children on the street! I can't think of myself when I am there. I have to put myself aside because I'm trying to save them Tsionie! All those young people with brilliant minds, with potential that will never be fulfilled. I'm trying to save them from drowning! Don't you see them drowning in the sea? Drowning to get here Tsionie? They look to me. I have to do my part. You are always in my heart, you both are. But every single day that God sends I'm fighting to save lives over there.

TSION. Is this what you wanted to tell us?

(Beat.)

SOLOMON. Everything I build, everything I make, I make for you. For all for you; my children. I want you to always know that. The house I built for you is now a Church.

TSION. A Church?

SOLOMON. A Church and a house of refuge for those in need. I want to give them shelter but there is not enough space inside. At night every inch of that house is covered in mattresses. We give them food...water and we share their hunger. But more people are outside every day and they need shelter. But we cannot build or extend there without your permission /...

YOSI. Our permission?

SOLOMON. I built that house in your name. In all your names. I wanted you to have something...somewhere to go back to...your mother and I even foolishly thought your brother could be there. But it was too late for him. Still, we can save lives with that house. That house should be a house of God, a house of Life! If I have your permission we can build and extend so the house becomes the Church that can also shelter people.

TSION. Why didn't you just take him with you?

SOLOMON. Ah, I tried... He never listened to me... that boy he... God forgive me... he never listened...

YOSI. Yo, come on fam! You think man like Ife would have juss got on the plane?

TSION. I'm juss / sayin'

YOSI. He woulda been clucking for them rocks brevs, imagine tryin' to get him on the plane?! Man couldn't even get on a bus without some madness kicking off!

TSION. I'm juss sayin' it would have been good for him. Being there. It might have saved him, innit.

SOLOMON. We can save others in his name.

YOSI. Say no more innit Dad. We got you.

SOLOMON. You know you can come and stay in the house any time you want, for as long as you want. It is still your house. It will always be your house.

YOSI. Come on Dad man, of course we support you! Why you even asking? Do your thing innit.

SOLOMON. God bless you son.

YOSI. You know what Dad, next summer I'm gonna come out there and volunteer you get me? I can even help with the build and that innit.

SOLOMON. God bless you both.

(**SOLOMON** *leafs through some papers in his document holder and slides some papers across to* **YOSI** *and* **TSION** *with a pen. He points to the signature areas on the papers...*)

SOLOMON. There and there. You just have to sign there and there.

(**YOSI** *signs the papers quickly, without reading anything and hands the pen to* **TSION**. *She hesitates. She doesn't sign.*)

TSION. I don't read Amharic.

SOLOMON. It's just the standard letter they use over there, it just says you give permission for the building works, that's all.

TSION. I know, but like I need to actually be able to read something before I sign it.

YOSI. Just sign it man.

TSION. Bruv you don't even speak Amharic let alone read it so shut your mouth!

YOSI. Oi, who you chatting to?

SOLOMON. It's just a simple / letter of permission Tsionie.

TSION. I need to be able to read it first.

SOLOMON. I can read it for you.

TSION. No, not now I feel like I'm being / pressured.

YOSI. Come on man! Why you making a big / ting out of it?

TSION. Like pressured into / signing it.

SOLOMON. No, no pressure Tsionie.

YOSI. *(To* **TSION**.*)* Why you buggin' out? Just sign it bruv!

SOLOMON. Son please!

YOSI. Proper bugging out boy!

TSION. I just... / I...

SOLOMON. No no no no, it's okay. Take all the time you need Tsionie.

    (Beat.)

TSION. Aida needs to see this too doesn't she?

SOLOMON. That's why I asked her to be here Tsionie, but okay, we'll show her. We can sit down with her and go through it if you / like?

TSION. Yeah. It just... it doesn't feel right to do this without her.

SOLOMON. That's what I told her. I told her it is a very important discussion but she is still not here, Tsionie. But, I understand. / I

TSION. I'm sorry Dad. I just think it's better if we go through it / together.

SOLOMON. Ah no! Don't apologise! We'll speak to her. I'll walk you both through this thing when we speak to her. Okay?

    (Beat.)

But, it's very important that we keep this between us, eh? We have to protect your mother. She always thought your brother would be in that house. The mention of it will break her heart.

7.

*(It is two a.m. the following morning. **AIDA** has passed out on the floor. Her hands are splattered in paint as are her clothes. A wine bottle is tipped over next to her. **SOLOMON** enters the space and goes to get himself a glass of water. He sees **AIDA** on the floor and quickly goes to see if she is okay. He wraps his dressing gown around his waist and goes to lift her. He struggles but manages to lift her. **AIDA** stirs but does not wake.)*

*(**SOLOMON** carries **AIDA** in his arms. He gently rests her on the couch and catches his breath. He disappears to another room and comes back out with fresh sheets. He takes off **AIDA**'s shoes and gently covers her with the sheets. He carefully places a cushion under her head. He covers her feet with the sheet and perches on the arm of the couch, watching his daughter silently as she sleeps.)*

8.

(Sunrise, first light.)

*(**AIDA** is outside working on her painting of Ife which is now more complete. **MERON** appears at the window, she sees **AIDA** and makes her way outside.)*

MERON. What are you doing out here at this time?

AIDA. I couldn't work in there.

*(**MERON** looks at Aida's painting.)*

AIDA. I want to paint him before the...without the...but / I...

(Beat.)

MERON. It is beautiful.

(Beat.)

AIDA. He was beautiful you know. The girls loved him at school.

(Beat.)

One summer, I think we must have been in year ten, me and some of the girls were on the grass near the bandstand on the Heath, and Ife was there, up on the bandstand. It was a hot summer like this, he was there, with his shirt open, holding onto the railing, one arm stretched out to the sky like he could reach it, like he was flying...and the sky was so blue that day, the gold chain he was wearing was glowing in the sun and he looked so free...so beautiful...all the girls were just gawking up at him and it was so awkward seeing them look at him like that. But I was proud. Proud that he was my brother...

(Beat.)

He never knew that though. When I told him he never believed me. He never knew how much I loved him.

MERON. He was loved. He was always loved.

AIDA. I want to paint him like that but all I keep seeing is him lying there on that thing... his skin kind of blue and those wounds... laying there like he starved to death, just skin and bone on that metal thing... that's all I keep seeing /...

MERON. I could see he wasn't eating, when he did, he'd never sit, he'd pace around by the window like a fugitive. I would ask him to stay, to sit, but they were always calling him. His body was wasting away but he'd never want to eat. To see him like that... who thought we would come here and he would starve...

(Beat.)

But he did eat something the last time he was here. Before he spoke to his father on the phone, he ate something. I'd made doro wot that day. You like doro wot, you both always loved doro wot. It was like he was a child again when he sat in there eating. I don't know what came over me, but I came out here and cried so he wouldn't hear me.

(Beat.)

AIDA. You shouldn't have to carry all that on your own.

MERON. God gives me strength.

AIDA. Dad should have been here supporting you.

MERON. Aida / please

AIDA. I'm not going to pretend anymore Mum!

MERON. Aida, / don't.

AIDA. Why do you let him use you like this?

MERON. It's not what you think. He will be gone the day after tomorrow.

AIDA. He shouldn't even be staying in this house.

MERON. How would it look if I didn't open the door for him when he came to bury his son.

> *(Beat.)*

It was the right thing to do.

AIDA. So, it's just about doing the right thing? What were you doing with him the other day then?

> *(Beat.)*

I saw you Mum!

MERON. That anger is not going to do you any good.

AIDA. Look what he did to you Mum, look what he did to Ife! Now he wants to come here act like he's still your husband?

MERON. He's still your father.

> *(Beat.)*

AIDA. I couldn't even speak for him.

> *(Beat.)*

He's haunting me you know Mum.

MERON. It's the grief that has filled our house. It is the grief that is everywhere. I turn and look for him. I stand at the window and wait for him. But he is gone. My boy is gone, but he is at peace now. That is all that matters now. The sun has to set on all of us one day, so we have to live. Honour your brother by living. Living and living well.

AIDA. He is not at peace. I can feel it.

MERON. He is at peace. Finally at / peace.

AIDA. He's not Mum. He can never be at peace until we all face what happened to him.

MERON. We can't change the past.

AIDA. But we have to face it. We have to face what happened to Ife.

9.

(Later on. A humid late morning.)

*(**TSION** prepares breakfast for the family. **YOSI**, who has a notepad under his arm, tinkers with an old fan which starts and soon stops again. **YOSI** is frustrated. He goes over to the windows and tries to yank them open.)*

TSION. Oi, leave them man.

YOSI. It's fucking boiling.

TSION. You're gonna break it bruv, leave it.

YOSI. Some dumb design ya know! How they making windows that don't even open properly?!

TSION. To stop people from jumping out innit.

YOSI. We're on the ground floor / fam.

TSION. Same thing to them. Same block.

YOSI. Can't fuckin' breathe in here / man!

TSION. It don't matter what floor you live / on.

YOSI. Ya know what I'm sayin' fam? When it's cold they go on like it's a big ting to fix the boiler and now it's hot they don't wanna sort out these stupid windows! Violations fam!

TSION. I've called them bare times but all they say is they'll look into it.

YOSI. Them lot are juss on taking the piss!

TSION. Overstretched innit.

YOSI. Pagans. They're always on some double speak ting!

TSION. I know!

YOSI. And fam, have you clocked how bare estates have mad names?

TSION. Bruv, you need to stop blazing in the mornings.

>   (YOSI *jots down lyrics on his note pad like he is having bursts of inspiration.*)

TSION. Breakfast is almost ready fam, can you stop doodling and go wake them up.

>   (*Enter* AIDA.)

AIDA. Is he up yet?

TSION. What?

AIDA. Dad, is he up yet?

YOSI. He was looking to chat to you ya know.

AIDA. About what?

TSION. He wants us to sign some papers or something, something about the house back home. That's why I was belling / you.

AIDA. He wants us to sign papers?

TSION. He said he'll chat to us about it today before he leaves.

YOSI. It's a charity ting innit. Man's setting up a charity ting out / there.

TSION. He needs to use the house there.

AIDA. Did you lot sign?

TSION. He did.

YOSI. I'm gonna go next summer and work with Dad innit.

TSION. I didn't sign coz it was in Amharic, but he said he'll take both of us through it properly. You hungry?

AIDA. Nah, I'm fine.

TSION. You should eat / fam.

YOSI. A vegan *wot* for you and real food for everybody else brevs!

TSION. You're a pagan man.

YOSI. What?

TSION. Most of Ethiopian food is vegan! Bruv, all of this *is* vegan!

YOSI. Is it?

> (**YOSI** *gets up and goes to the kitchen area.*)

TSION. Fam, you can't be moving that ignant 'bout your own culture ya get me?

YOSI. Shut up man! What you think you're bad coz you made some injera?

> (**YOSI** *grabs a piece of injera and darts across the room, giggling.*)

TSION. Watch when I catch you bruv!

> (**YOSI** *goes back to writing his lyrics.*)

YOSI. *(Rapping to himself.)* Man movin' like Menelik, touch Yard to heal the needy and the sick, uh. *(To* **AIDA**.*)* Oi you wanna hear my new / barz?

AIDA. Not now Yosi / man.

YOSI. *(Back to working out his lyrics to himself.)* Son of a prophet, son of a preacher, son of a / priest uh

TSION. *(Shouting across the room as she lays the table.)* MUM, DAD! BREAKFAST! *(To* **YOSI**.*)* Oi Yosh?

YOSI. *(Still writing.)* One sec.

AIDA. DAD! BREAKFAST IS READY!

YOSI. *(Rapping to himself.)* No niggers in Africa / yeah-yeah

AIDA. *(To* **TSION**.*)* Is he still asleep?

TSION. I dunno. Can you go check fam?

AIDA. DAD!

YOSI. *(Still working on his lyrics.)* From that red earth a truth / saya

AIDA. Yosi?

YOSI. Armed with a dreamers / prayer

AIDA. *(To* **YOSI.***)* What's wrong with you?

YOSI. What's wrong with me? Fam, I ain't the one rolling in here at four in the morning, waved off that molly and chatting shit about seeing ghosts / and

AIDA. When did I ever say anything to you about seeing ghosts?

YOSI. You don't think I can't hear you through them walls bruv?

TSION. *(Finishing laying the table.)* MUM! DAD! ARE YOU COMING?

YOSI. Nah, levels yeah, instead of worrying about Ife, you need to be thinking about going to rehab yourself / fam

AIDA. Yosi, shut the fuck up!

TSION. Yosh man, leave it bruv!

AIDA. Why you being like this?

YOSI. I'm juss being real ya get me!

AIDA. Don't fucking start with me today!

　　　　*(**MERON** enters.)*

MERON. What's all this noise?

TSION. It's Yosh.

MERON. Ah! You are arguing with your sisters when you should be helping them? / Eh?

YOSI. Sorry Mummy.

MERON. I don't want you arguing with them here today, you hear me?

(**SOLOMON** *enters.*)

SOLOMON. *(Using an Amharic expression of surprise.)* Erah! Erah! Erah! Endeah? Anchi?! Is this Tsionie making this food, eh?

TSION. Have a seat Dad.

SOLOMON. Eh! Look at this! You make this?! Oooooohweee, the smell! *(To the others.)* That aroma of home! Ah! It made me get up and get ready like a young man on his birthday! Eeeeeh? Tsionie! Look at you! An excellent young woman cooking like this!

TSION. It's nothing Dad, it's / simple it's

SOLOMON. Aida? Come on, join us! Let us give thanks!

(**AIDA** *joins the family around the table. The food is neatly laid. The family stand in a circle, holding hands with their heads bowed apart from* **AIDA** *whose head is raised and her eyes are open.*)

Heavenly Father, we want to thank you for bringing us together in this difficult time and providing us with this sustenance. Thank you for guiding us and carrying us through these trials and tribulations. Give us the strength to serve you Lord, and to live for you. Guide these children, walk with them and keep them in your light Dear Lord, and bless this food, bless this nourishment so that we can continue living in service of You. In Jesus' name, amen.

ALL. *(Apart from* **AIDA.***)* Amen.

(*They settle down in their seats and start eating.* **AIDA** *does not touch her food, her attention is on* **SOLOMON. SOLOMON** *eats quickly and hungrily as does* **YOSI.***)*

SOLOMON. Ah! Tsionie! This is delicious! Where did you learn cooking like this, eh?

MERON. Huh! This foolish man! Where do you think, / eh?

SOLOMON. *(Exaggerated appreciation of the food.)* Ooooooooohweeeeeee! Ah! Tsionie! They don't even make injera like this in Addis! I'm telling you!

(TSION sits and starts eating.)

(To AIDA.) You're not eating?

AIDA. I'm not hungry.

(Beat.)

I couldn't speak for Ife at the funeral... I... I... I didn't have the words then... but I wrote this and I wanted to share it with you...

(Beat.)

AIDA. ...Since we're all here now... and Dad, you're going back to Addis tomorrow so I... I thought I should share it with you now... I... it's... I'll just read / it...

YOSI. What? Ah, come on / fam!

TSION. Yosh man!

(AIDA takes out a piece of paper, unfolds it and takes a moment before reading it out loud.)

AIDA. Ife, Ashenafi, my brother, my twin... when you're a twin... it's like a part of you is always out there. Out there where your twin is. My twin brother was so beautiful. I was lucky to have been born with him. Lucky to have shared a womb with him. He made a way for me. Five minutes before me. Made my path easier. He always did. He saw the world was worth coming into and I followed him out. I loved him. Loved him even then. And I love him now. I will always love / him.

SOLOMON. Yes. God rest his / soul.

AIDA. It was hard...hard to see what the drugs did to him. I felt powerless. It was like watching someone drowning when you don't know how to swim.

> *(Beat.)*

I thought he'd get through it though. I thought he would recover and we would return to how we were. Me and him. Ife and Aida. I thought we'd dance again... that was what we did...that was our language... that was our secret...but I was wrong... I got to survive but my brother didn't...

SOLOMON. Ah, Aida, Aida, Aidiyay. Come, / sit, eat.

AIDA. Recently, I've wondered if he was the sacrifice for all of us. A sacrifice for our new life here.

YOSI. Fam, it's done now yeah, why you draggin' / it?

AIDA. Let me finish Yosi / man!

YOSI. Just because you feel a way 'bout bouncing on him, don't mean you have to come here and make us feel the same / yeah.

AIDA. *(To* **YOSI.***)* You couldn't even acknowledge him when you saw him on road / and now

YOSI. Couldn't acknowledge him? Bruv, you're the one that cut out / yeah

MERON. Yosiyas, have some respect!

YOSI. Nah, Mum, she's coming here and all tryin' to bait / us out!

AIDA. He was my twin. My twin, yeah. What do you know about losing / your twin?

YOSI. You ain't the only one that's lost him fam. You cut out and we had to deal with the madness. All the crackhead shit he would do every time he came here, we had to deal with that yeah. He come in here lookin' like the walking dead fam, like a zombie with sunken eyes and missing teeth and let Mum see him like that every time. Let us all see him like that. Innit T? What you think it was all happy families? That shit used to scare me fam. / What he did to himself.

SOLOMON. / *(Wanting to comfort* YOSI.*)* Ah, Yosi, Yosiyas, son...

YOSI. What? Where were you when feds were rolling up in our yard and gripsing me up, looking for him coz he was always stealing some shit? Where were you when these Crescent hoodrats were booting down our door coz he owed them money and he didn't even live here? Man even came through one time and stole the Nintendo Wii Mum got for me for Christmas. I was only ten but he took it anyway. That's what he was on. Fuckeries.

Everyone in endz knew that crackhead running round the block naked was my brother! I've had to grow up with that yeah. He never gave a fuck about us. He'd even bring his crackhead friends in here to smoke when we were just kids fam!

TSION. Fam, it's true.

YOSI. You know what I'm sayin' T!

SOLOMON. What?!

TSION. He'd come here off his head and start stripping in the courtyard out there, in front of the whole estate fam. People filming him on their phones out their windows but he didn't care. Even when even when me and Yosh begged him to stop, he never listened. He'd juss carry on like he had to do it, like he had to prove a point until someone called the police or chased him / out.

YOSI. No one forced him to smoke crack. He chose to do that. He was supposed to be my big bro and I see Mum cry about him all the time. He brought the madness to our door step when he should have been there to protect us, so don't try it. *(Gesturing to* **TSION**.*)* If it was her yeah, if it was her, I'd never cut out on her like you cut / out on him!

MERON. Yosiyas! Enough! Don't speak to your sister / like that!

SOLOMON. *(Supporting* **YOSI**.*)* He is right. The boy is / right.

AIDA. You should have told me.

SOLOMON. *(To* **AIDA**.*)* Listen to your brother and sister. There was no drugs and drinking in this house until your brother brought it in here, these shameful things!

YOSI. All coming here and tryin' to air us out you / know!

AIDA. I'm not airing you out, I'm talking about Dad and what happen to / Ife!

SOLOMON. *(To* **AIDA**.*)* You are smoking and drinking too, eh? You think I don't know?

AIDA. If it was like that for you two, you should have said.

SOLOMON. *(To* **AIDA**.*)* You have to be a good example to your brother and sister now, eh?

TSION. Fam, you were in another country or busy, always too busy / innit.

SOLOMON. *(To* **AIDA**.*)* Think about them. You are the eldest now, you have to lead a clean life, a Godly life and they will / follow!

YOSI. All coming here tryin' to lecture us! Move from me / man!

AIDA. *(To* YOSI *and* TSION.*)* I should have done better for you both. I know, but you have to know what happed to Ife when we came here.

YOSI. Aida, I said move from me!

SOLOMON. We brought you here to give you the life we only dreamed of. We brought you here so you could be educated men and women who will one day go back and be a light to our / people.

MERON. *(To* SOLOMON.*)* Ah! You are still dreaming. We got here and we didn't even know how to speak to them anymore, we didn't know the ways here or / the

SOLOMON. *(To* AIDA.*)* This is the land that God has truly blessed and we gave it to you. Both of you. Your mother / and I

MERON. *(To* SOLOMON.*)* Don't fool yourself. God knows how hard it was coming here and learning to live again, but it was harder for them. They grew up in our confusion here.

SOLOMON. They had everything they needed here! We gave them everything they / needed!

MERON. It was too hard here! The way we were treated – this country was never meant to be a home for us!

AIDA. Dad, did Ife have everything he needed?

MERON. We put every penny into trying to get that house ready so we could go back. We were breaking apart / here!

AIDA. Ife was alone in some hostel at sixteen!

SOLOMON. I didn't make Ashenafi leave home. That wasn't / me.

MERON. I had to protect him, that's why I asked them to give him a / hostel.

SOLOMON. That is when we lost him.

TSION. Mum, you kicked him out?

YOSI. Rah...

MERON. He was only supposed to be in that hostel until we could take him back to Ethiopia, until that house was ready.

YOSI. Nah, that is peak Mum.

SOLOMON. Let's not dwell on this now, eh?

MERON. God forgive me for putting him out of this house, but I didn't know what else to do! I thought he would be safer there than he was in here.

SOLOMON. (*To* MERON.) You made him leave this house. You did that. That is when we lost him for / good.

MERON. STOP! JUST STOP! LET ME MOURN MY SON IN PEACE!

> (*Beat.*)

I just want some peace now. Just a little peace instead of all this blame!

> (*Beat.*)

> (SOLOMON *returns to eating.*)

AIDA. It was you Dad. He had to leave this house because of / you.

SOLOMON. That's enough / now.

AIDA. Because of the way you treated / him...

SOLOMON. Listen to your mother. We want peace is this house now, eh?

AIDA. He ended up dying on the streets without anything, he didn't even have any / shoes!

SOLOMON. Aida, please stop / this!

TSION. He had no shoes?

SOLOMON. He wasn't a child.

    (Beat.)

He could have made something of himself like you all have here, / but

AIDA. Here, he ended up begging on the street / Dad.

SOLOMON. He had the same opportunities you had, educated among the white children like you. He had everything he needed here, but he chose the pavement instead! We gave him / everything!

AIDA. You couldn't even get us a pair of shoes when we got here!

SOLOMON. Eh? Meron, do you hear this? We didn't give him shoes?

AIDA. No, / you

SOLOMON. The boy was sick. He was ill. We tried. You think I didn't try to show him all the love in my heart? I was cleaning shit and vomit so he could be someone. You think I didn't love him? He was my first born son. I named him even before he was born. I wanted him even before he came into this world.

AIDA. You don't hit the people you love Dad.

SOLOMON. I hit you when you were doing something that will harm you. I hit you to stop you. To help / you.

AIDA. Did you hitting Ife help him?

SOLOMON. Are you saying that I caused Ife to do what he did? Is that what you are saying?

AIDA. The only shoes me and Ife ever got was from some giveaway pile anyway. Barbie shoes! Ife took them shoes out of that pile like he found treasure. He didn't even know what Barbie was, he just liked the colours and the way the rhinestones sparkled. He went to school the next day thinking he would be like the other kids but they all laughed at him. They all laughed at him and his Barbie shoes. He came home and tried ripping out the rhinestones but you saw him do that and you punched him in / the face.

SOLOMON. Ahhhhhhh please, please, please, I don't what to hear this anymore!

YOSI. What do you mean punched him in the face / fam?

AIDA. Every time Dad came home he was always pushing him around. Throwing him against the wall. Beating him up. That's what he did. You lot just don't remember coz you were too young, *(To* **YOSI**.*)* you weren't even born.

SOLOMON. I'm not answering this thing. She's upset.

AIDA. It's the truth though Dad, isn't it?

SOLOMON. Sometimes when people fail in life they want to find someone to blame. *(To* **AIDA**.*)* Be sure daughter. If you are accusing me of these disgusting things be /sure.

MERON. She is not accusing you! She is telling you the / truth!

SOLOMON. What truth? That I smacked him a few times to help / him?

AIDA. You abused him!

SOLOMON. Abuse! Ah, you are listening to the language you hear now in the street eh? This Godless government say "abuse" and the child can send you to prison for something so silly! You are smacking the child to make him behave! To help him! Abuse, eh? Read your Bible instead. Foolishness is bound up in the heart of a child, but the rod of discipline will drive it far from him. Proverbs 22:15.

TSION. Dad, you can't keep using religion as an excuse! Hitting a child like that is abuse!

YOSI. Dad clips me around the head all the time. It's not that deep fam.

SOLOMON. Go back home and see how the children are disciplined.

AIDA. Yeah, breaking his nose is disciplining him / was it?

YOSI. What?!

SOLOMON. He did that to himself.

AIDA. Oh yeah, he flung himself against the wall, is that what you're saying?

SOLOMON. You didn't see half of it! That boy he was always ready to harm / himself!

TSION. Dad, did you break Ife's nose?

SOLOMON. I didn't break anybody's nose. He had an accident.

AIDA. You did that to him coz you came home one day and saw him dancing. His t-shirt looked like it was dipped in blood!

YOSI. What the fuck?!

SOLOMON. Shameful! This is / shameful!

AIDA. No, you shamed Ife for being who he was. For wanting to love who he loved. For being the son you / never wanted.

SOLOMON. Shhhhhh stop this now. Stop this!

MERON. *(To* **SOLOMON**.*)* You were always jealous, jealous of his curious mind, of his brilliant / mind.

SOLOMON. *(To* **MERON**.*)* You prayed to change him too! Did you forget?

*(**YOSI** starts pacing, he is distressed.)*

TSION. / Yosh?

YOSI. Nah, this is / fucked!

TSION. Fam? Fam? You alright?

YOSI. Why don't no one ever tell me nothing?!

MERON. You have to face up to it Solomon. You drove the boy / to despair.

YOSI. This is pissing me off fam.

SOLOMON. Despair? What despair? I buried my own dreams and willed him to fly but he threw it back in my face! Don't talk to me about despair! Everything / I did

TSION. Yosh, fam, it's okay.

YOSI. *(To TSION.)* Stop trying to fix everything!

MERON. We came here for ourselves Solomon. You left us. You promised to prepare the house for Ife but you went there to womanize instead!

(TSION exits.)

SOLOMON. Everything I did, I did / for them!

AIDA. Fucking narcissist.

YOSI. Oi, watch your mouth fam!

AIDA. Shut up!

SOLOMON. Don't speak to me like this! You are still my own flesh and blood!

AIDA. You're a liar!

(TSION returns holding Solomon's leather document holder behind her.)

SOLOMON. Tsionie, you are sensible, speak to her. Tell her I'm telling the truth.

TSION. Are you Dad?

(Beat.)

TSION. *(Revealing the document.)* Mum, Dad asked us to sign this yesterday.

SOLOMON. What are you doing Tsionie?

TSION. It's about the house back home. He was asking me and Yosh to sign / it.

SOLOMON. Tsionie! Please, leave that. Put it back. Please, put it / back!

> **(MERON** *takes the document holder from* **TSION** *and starts looking through the papers.)*

SOLOMON. Meron... Meron... I wanted to talk to you first / but I

MERON. Did you sign this?

TSION. No, it was just Yosh who signed it.

MERON. *(To* **YOSI.***)* Why didn't you come to me with this?

YOSI. He's turning the house into a church. Innit / Dad?

SOLOMON. We could make a great Church in Ashenanfi's name.

YOSI. He's trying to help and shelter people there Mum.

MERON. This is a transfer of ownership from all of you to him.

AIDA. Wow!

YOSI. Yo, Dad?

TSION. He's a liar Yosh. He's been lying to us about everything.

AIDA. Transfer of ownership?

MERON. These last eight years I've brought them up on my own, without a penny from you, now you want to take away that house from / them?

SOLOMON. It's not like that. Let me / explain.

TSION. Dad, you literally said it was a permission to /extend.

SOLOMON. It's the only paperwork they gave / me.

TSION. Pressuring me to sign even though you knew?

SOLOMON. It is still yours.

AIDA. That house was meant for us! For Ife!

SOLOMON. The house will always be yours.

MERON. *(To* **SOLOMON.***)* You've moved her in there haven't you? They are in the house that was meant for my son.

YOSI. What? Yo, Dad? Is that true?

TSION. Obviously it's true fam, she just said.

SOLOMON. It is not like that Meron. I'm doing God's work there.

YOSI. Swear down, if that's true / Dad

TSION. *(To* **YOSI.***)* Yosh? Fam?

AIDA. Dad, tell the truth about what happened to Ife / and

YOSI. I'm gonna switch!

SOLOMON. Get away from me you serpent!

TSION. Yosh?

AIDA. What does the Bible say? / "If we confess our sins, He is faithful and will forgive us of all our sins and purify us from all unrighteousness." See? Apologise! For all of it!

SOLOMON. Ah! The devil can quote scripture too!

YOSI. What the fuck is wrong with this family!

AIDA. Apologise to Ife!

SOLOMON. Apologise for what? For giving you life?

YOSI. Swear, I'm gonna go psycho in a / minute!

TSION. Yosh, just breathe / fam.

AIDA. Apologise so he can be at peace! Look at me! He can hear you! I promise, Ife can hear / you!

SOLOMON. All the sacrifices I made for you, and you dare spit in my face like this! Viper!

AIDA. My brother is dead because of you! Apologise for what you did to him!

> (**SOLOMON** *slaps* **AIDA** *with the back of his hand so forcefully that it sends her reeling to the floor.* **MERON** *lets out a wail in terror and rushes to* **AIDA**. *Both* **TSION** *and* **MERON** *shield* **AIDA** *from* **SOLOMON**. **YOSI** *leaps in and grabs* **SOLOMON** *by the collar and pins him to the wall, overpowering him. The boy is now the man.)*

MERON. DON'T TOUCH HER! DON'T YOU DARE TOUCH / HER!

YOSI. Yo, what you doin'? What the fuck you think you're / doing?

TSION. *(To* **AIDA**.*)* Are you alright? Aida?

> (**TSION** *continues to ask,* **AIDA** *is reeling and in shock. Her responses to* **TSION** *barely audible.)*

SOLOMON. Ah, Aida! Aidiyay, I'm sorry. I'm sorry. I'm so / sorry. Son. Ah, / son...

YOSI. What, you think you can come here and violate us like / this?!

SOLOMON. Son, please...

> (**SOLOMON** *struggles to move but* **YOSI** *is too strong and suddenly* **SOLOMON** *seems weak and fragile.)*

MERON. Get out! I'm not going to let you destroy the rest of my children like you destroyed my son! / Get out!

> (**YOSI** *presses his forehead against his father's, torn between his rage and his desperate longing for his father's love.*)

YOSI. You're supposed to be my dad.

> (**MERON** *and* **TSION** *pull* **YOSI** *away.*)

SOLOMON. I'm sorry! Son, please, I'm sorry!

YOSI. *(To* **SOLOMON.***)* Nah! You're a fucking liar!

SOLOMON. Tsionie? Please?

TSION. I've got nothing to say to you anymore Dad!

SOLOMON. Son?

MERON. Get away from him!

SOLOMON. Son?

YOSI. YOU'RE SUPPOSED TO BE MY DAD!

SOLOMON. Son, please!

YOSI. Move from me man! Don't touch me! Don't fucking touch me!

SOLOMON. Meron? Ah! God forgive me! Oh, God forgive / me!

MERON. *(To* **SOLOMON.***)* You will never have that house. As long as I live, I will not let you take that house away from them. Get out of my home!

> (**SOLOMON** *leaves the room.*)

10.

(AIDA enters Tsion's room. She sees SOLOMON cowering there, trying to hide.)

SOLOMON. It's not too late for us to start again...it's not too late, is it Aida?

AIDA. You shouldn't be here anymore Dad.

SOLOMON. Please stay.

AIDA. He better not find you in here.

(SOLOMON is distraught.)

SOLOMON. Stay. Please. Stay. I did not get a chance to explain to you.

AIDA. There's nothing left to explain Dad.

SOLOMON. I only wanted to do some good. Ah! I only wanted to be of some use Aida.

AIDA. You still can. You can still help the people there Dad.

SOLOMON. We should have never left, Aida. We were happy back home, weren't we? We were happy back then, me, you, your mother and your brother. We were happy there. We didn't need anything else, did we? That shack was enough for us, wasn't it? You and your brother had all that space outside. That garden. That endless garden. We were happy. Ah! But we came here and we lost him. We lost him and we lost ourselves.

(Beat.)

Aida...daughter...please...

(Beat.)

Hold me.

AIDA. I can't.

SOLOMON. Please. Hold me.

AIDA. I can't. I'm sorry.

Epilogue

(A few days later.)

(A bright morning.)

(AIDA and YOSI are on the roof. YOSI has a spliff behind his ear and a note pad in his hand, he scribbles down lyrics with bursts of inspiration. AIDA looks out onto the estate.)

AIDA. I forgot how amazing this view was.

YOSI. Yeah, this roof is the spot innit!

AIDA. It was our spot... me and Ife's...

YOSI. Yo, / fam

AIDA. You can see Kite Hill from here and the bandstand.

YOSI. Fam, you wanna hear my barz?

AIDA. You've been writing yeah?

YOSI. Yeah, man's a lyricist out here!

AIDA. Is it yeah?

YOSI. Dun know.

AIDA. Go on then Yosh, let me hear you.

　　　　(Beat.)

YOSI. I ain't got no beat, but...

　　　　(Looks at his note pad for a moment, then...)

Son of a sinner, son of a saint

Son is a Rose from concrete, a child of fate

Son of dreamers, dreaming a dream that never came

Dreaming streets paved with gold but this concrete is
　　　the same

Still crossed the desert and parted seas

Drowned in this city and deferred their dreams to me

Somebody wake me, tell me where to from here

Take me back to the root and wash away my fear

Back to that earth, red red earth I never knew

When I get over there it's gonna make me brand new

And born again, an African on a higher plane

Praying to Black Jesus to keep me sane

An exile searching for the love that don't come, to visit these wretched slums

Spitting on the rooftop, to the beat of Emperor's drums

Through the wire, through the concrete and through the block

Screamin' Ashenafi forever, Ashenafi my rock

AIDA. Rah! Yosh!

YOSI. Yeah.

AIDA. Yosh man you're propa talented you know!

YOSI. Ah, love fam.

>   (*Beat.*)

YOSI. Yo? When's your art ting coming on?

AIDA. End of the year.

YOSI. I'm gonna reach that still.

AIDA. It will be good to have you there Yosh.

YOSI. Yeah, I'll come with T innit.

AIDA. Yeah.

>   (**TSION** *joins them on the roof. She has a lighter in her hand and a plastic bag with Ife's possessions.*)

TSION. Is this where you lot are?

AIDA. Yeah.

TSION. I don't know what to do with all this.

YOSI. Man lived light boy. Just a lighter and some garms.

AIDA. That's all he had.

TSION. *(Playing with the lighter.)* What do you lot wanna do with his stuff?

YOSI. No point holding on to them things there.

AIDA. I'll keep it.

> *(Beat.)*

He's free now.

> *(Beat.)*

He's free.

> *(YOSI takes the lighter from TSION and lights his spliff. He gives the lighter to AIDA.)*

AIDA. Oi Yosh, let me get in on that yeah.

YOSI. Yeah, calm.

> *(YOSI takes a puff and passes the spliff to AIDA.)*

AIDA. Safe.

TSION. She's gonna smell that on you ya know.

YOSI. It's fine T. She ain't gonna be back from Church for a while. You want some?

> *(Beat.)*

TSION. Ah, go on then.

> *(YOSI passes TSION the spliff, she takes a drag, coughs and passes it back to YOSI.)*

TSION. Thanks.

YOSI. Cool.

> *(They smoke together in silence, listening to the hum of the city, each in their own thought as they continue to share the spliff with each other.)*

> *(Lights fade.)*

The End

Lightning Source UK Ltd.
Milton Keynes UK
UKHW022153200522
403332UK00002B/3